T0194748

THE TREASURE IS THE TRIP

The Journey Has Its Rewards

*A personal story of one girl learning
how to trip the light fantastic*

P. J. Brown

WESTBOW
PRESS®
A DIVISION OF THOMAS NELSON
& ZONDERVAN

WestBow Press books may be ordered through
booksellers or by contacting:

WestBow Press
A Division of Thomas Nelson & Zondervan
1663 Liberty Drive
Bloomington, IN 47403
www.westbowpress.com
1 (866) 928-1240

ISBN: 978-1-9736-1379-4 (sc)
ISBN: 978-1-9736-1381-7 (hc)
ISBN: 978-1-9736-1380-0 (e)

Library of Congress Control Number: 2018900292

Print information available on the last page.

WestBow Press rev. date: 04/24/2018

I dedicate this book to those
who may be searching
for
a little more understanding.

I want to thank
my dear husband, Spencer, who loved
the Lord and me, in that order,
.   and
our five wonderful children, who have taught me
so much and helped me so much and without
whom I would not have been able to get this far,
and
my sister, who was there for me and still is.

And most of all I thank Jesus, my Savior and Friend.

PREFACE

Some months after my son's accident and life had
quieted somewhat, I realized that the unusual
incidents involved needed to be recorded before
they were forgotten, and I began writing the story as
I remembered. Later, I decided that there were other
happenings in my life that were meaningful, and
perhaps I should incorporate them into the writing and
make a history for my kids and grandkids to read, and
maybe something I had learned could benefit others.
The story of the accident is from my point of view; my
son gave me permission to publish it, understanding
that God is perfect though we are not, and if this story
can be of benefit in anyone's life, God will use it.

INTRODUCTION

There have been books written and movies made telling the adventures of people on a treasure hunt. It is believed that the finding of the treasure will be the end of all and will make the hunters happy beyond expectations. They have a map with directions, sometimes coded, and a guide to make sure they are on the right track, because they may have to go to faraway places and meet many obstacles on their journey.

We ran a commercial cleaning business, and when it was not quite two years old, we bought a computer and the software we needed to run it. It was a DOS-based computer, and the only experience I had prior to a keyboard was a typewriter. I was green. I paid for an expert in the software we had selected to come to my office and sit in a chair right next to me and teach me everything I would need to know to run the business on this computer. I had twenty hours to learn four different programs. Somehow, we managed to get through three-quarters of the task when my expensive teaching was done. I sure wished I had him there on a daily basis when my first payroll was ready to get out, but I couldn't afford any more time. I have made mistakes over the years and had to pay an accountant to correct it. It was an adventure.

I guess that most of us are looking for the treasure and want to get there and retire from struggling and just enjoy. Even Christians, who have the directions and the guide, still have the mind-set that the treasure is the most important thing. But I have found that most of us are looking for a treasure, and it's the adventure that is most important. The treasure is the trip. The destination is heaven, which is in God's hands, but the trip is in our hands. We have the directions, the Word of God, and we have the guide, which is the Holy Spirit; we will get to our destination, but will God get the glory in our trip? Can you imagine anyone foolish enough to consider themselves smart enough to try to make the trip without reading the directions or moving out without the guide? I did exactly that. I thought living was a natural thing and everyone seemed to be doing okay, so I would just follow my instincts and check out the guidebook when necessary. After quite a few years and a number of errors of judgment, my heavenly Father God had such compassion on me and that He brought to my attention, my need.

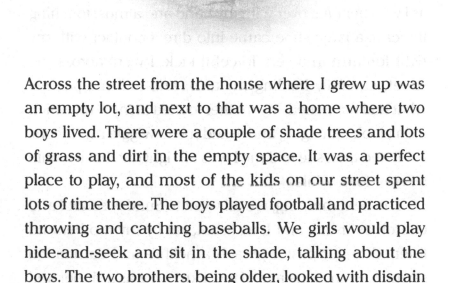

Across the street from the house where I grew up was an empty lot, and next to that was a home where two boys lived. There were a couple of shade trees and lots of grass and dirt in the empty space. It was a perfect place to play, and most of the kids on our street spent lots of time there. The boys played football and practiced throwing and catching baseballs. We girls would play hide-and-seek and sit in the shade, talking about the boys. The two brothers, being older, looked with disdain on us girls, but sometimes they played with us and some of the other kids who lived on our block.

One Saturday when I was ten years old, I think in May because school was still going on, we were playing Kick the Can in the empty lot—and I was "it." I felt pretty important because they had included me in the game. After closing my eyes and counting to ten, I cautiously opened my eyes and began my search for anyone I

1

could find so that I could make it to the can first. I soon discovered one of the brothers' hiding spot and was running as fast as my ten-year-old legs could go, but his stride was much longer than mine, and we reached the can at the same time. I desperately reached out my right arm to grab the can before it was kicked, but he got close enough to stretch his long leg out to give it a good kick; as I was bending over with my hand and almost touching the can, a large shoe came into direct contact with my right forearm in a very forceful kick. I went across the street, carefully holding my arm, and told my parents what had happened. My mother looked at my arm, which didn't look damaged, and asked me to wiggle my fingers; I did, and then she told me I was all right but that it would be sore for a while.

The next morning, we all went to Sunday school and church as usual, and I, as usual, sat by my mother and listened to our pastor preach a hellfire and damnation sermon. Even at the age of ten, I knew I was a sinner and bound for hell. My parents had caught me in numerous acts and punished me accordingly. Dad would sometimes make me cut a small branch off the tree in the backyard when I had been really disobedient, and then he would switch my legs, hoping I would remember the pain the next time I was tempted. I had even memorized passages in the Bible about lying and disobeying.

For sure I was a sinner, and that Sunday, hearing once again about God's judgment on sinners in hell, I responded to the call at the end of the service. The pastor counseled me and prayed with me as I, by faith, prayed to receive Jesus as my Savior. Along with some others who had come for prayer, I stood up front and waited to be welcomed into church membership by the congregation. My arm had been kicked just the day before, and it hurt even more after I had shaken the hands of about two hundred people after the service.

It ended up hurting so much that my dad decided to take me to the office of a doctor friend of his for x-rays. He told us that the larger bone was cracked about in the middle of my arm. It was too late for a cast; it had already begun healing. So, to this day, my right arm has a slight curve.

The following day, I went to school, and the only thing that had changed on the outside of me was my arm. It gave me something to talk about, but no one at school would guess that I had prayed to receive Christ as my Savior. And it went on like that for years. Yes, most chums knew I went to church regularly, but I didn't talk a lot about my faith. I was involved in many student activities and was regarded as a good girl because of the things I didn't do, but I was quiet about spiritual stuff.

Much later on in my life, when I started thinking seriously about my relationship with God, I tried to remember when I had actually become a believer, and then I realized that God had given me a painful memory, like a bookmark, to remind me when I became His child.

I am ever grateful for that kick, because it happened the day before my spiritual birthday.

Three comments have been made to me over the years that have made a difference in my life. The first one was when my mother came into my bedroom one morning as I was getting dressed for school; she had been wondering why it was taking so long. When I told her that I had been praying for God to let me know what to wear, she said to me that God wasn't interested in what I would wear. That went so against what I had been led to believe about God. There were so many stories in the Bible of God's involvement in people's lives down to the smallest detail. He even cared about the little sparrow, and His Word said that I was far more important than a sparrow. If I wore something immodest, I knew He would care. If I were dirty or unkempt, it would not be appropriate for a King's ambassador. And if what I wore distracted from my countenance where the light of God can be seen, He would care. This was too much for me to resolve that morning, but it did give me lots to think about.

The second comment was made at a vacation Bible school much later, when I was the leader over teenagers. One sixteen-year-old asked me a question about prayer, and my answer was to the effect that we are given the opportunity to cooperate with God. This young man, who had been raised in church, retorted back that we can't cooperate with God. I was taken aback at the thought that his view of God was rather like my mother's. Both saw God as distant and too involved over big issues to concern Himself with insignificant human stuff. Many instances I have said to my heavenly Father God, "Excuse me for bothering you again over this problem, but ..." Always, I am reassured in my spirit that it is okay with Him, because He is infinite and He infinitely loves me.

The third comment was from an interim preacher taking our pulpit one Sunday when our pastor was away. In the middle of his sermon, he explained John 17:3: "whom to know is eternal life," and it was so simple and outstanding that *knowing about* is very different than *knowing*. Knowing takes an ongoing relationship, a give and a take, and a listening and a talking.

In high school, I took Latin and science and math to prepare me for something in the medical field. I was leaning toward becoming a nurse, but my dad discouraged me since he had heard that nurses were "loose." My biology teacher had a friend who worked in the medical laboratory at a hospital in the area, and my teacher had been asked whether there were any senior students she would recommend to work in the lab after graduation. She recommended me and one other girl. It sounded really interesting to me, so after talking with my parents, I decided to make a visit and check it out. I thought it might be better than being a nurse.

I showed up one day and was taken on a tour of all the labs—hematology, serology, chemistry, bacteriology, and pathology. I had found the career I had been preparing for and loved it. Then I was hired. After working in the lab a couple of months, I decided that I wanted to be a registered technician; with the help of some coworkers, I chose a university in middle Tennessee and started my application. I would have to work to put myself through school, and I was directed to contact the hospital near the school to see if they would use a person with only three months of experience. They needed help too, and I was given a job. My hours would be 3 to 11 p.m., so I could attend classes.

I had saved enough money from the summer to cover my tuition, and I took the entrance exam and registered for school. My dad dropped me off at the hospital where I would have a room in the nurse's dorm. I am sure I asked God to help me get into school and get the job, but I don't know whether I remembered to thank Him. I just expected Him to work things out. I regularly assumed blessings from Him and presumed upon His goodness. That was my mode of operation.

I found a church and made every effort to get to worship services, but I don't remember ever giving an offering. I was putting myself through college and needed all I earned; that was my rationale, anyway.

The pastor's son, Mark, met me and asked me out on a date, and though he was nice and good-looking too, we just didn't hit it off. Some days later, I received a phone call from his best friend, Spencer, who told me that Mark suggested he call me. We talked for hours without a pause in between words. We hit it off on that call, and sometime later, Spencer told me that he had seen me sitting on a small rock wall near the university while I was waiting for the bus that would take me to the hospital. He had mentioned this to Mark, which prompted Mark to tell Spencer to give me a call. Spencer had also told his mom that he had seen the girl he was going to marry (I was totally unaware of this information when we started dating).

After a few weeks of seeing each other, we decided that we would go steady. The very next evening, Spencer called me to say that perhaps we were being too hasty. This hurt me and I angrily called off our planned dates for the weekend. He refused and insisted we go on as planned. He was surprised at my reaction and suggested that we just taper off and should see other people. I was rather offended and hung up.

The next morning, we were in chapel, and he followed me to my biology class and even got on the bus to the hospital with me to persuade me to forget about the call the night before. He gave me a poem he'd written: "I have gone with many, have liked a few, have loved but one, Pat that's you." That got to me, but I still waited to the end of the line when we arrived at the hospital to assure him that all was good.

Later, towards the end of November, both of us decided to quit seeing each other, but at Christmas, I received a card from him, to my surprise. He still thought about me. And in February, I woke up one morning remembering a dream I had the night before about him. I had to get to the university library early to research a paper I was writing; no one was on campus that early, except for Spencer, who I ran into as I was walking up the library steps. As I looked up, there he was, and it felt like the Lord dumped a load of love down on me at that very moment.

We started dating again and talking a bit of a more permanent relationship. His father was transferred to Knoxville that summer; we wrote long letters and spent a fortune on phone calls. At Christmas, he came for a visit, bringing me an engagement ring. We were married on Valentine's Day and moved to Knoxville. I never graduated or earned a registration as a medical technician, but married the man I believe God brought into my life. And I was able to work as a lab technician in hospitals every place we moved to, the first one in Knoxville.

Spencer, who is a natural-born salesman, began working for a national shoe store chain, and I worked at the hospital where our daughter, Christy, and first son, Jeremy, were born. Spencer did well and was transferred to the store in Washington DC, where we lived for about two years and then were moved to Royal Oak, Michigan, where we stayed for another two years and where number three, Andrew, was born.

From there, we went to Dayton, Ohio, where Christy started school and where Gordon, the fourth and, I thought, last child was born. The next promotion moved us to South Bend, Indiana, where I found myself in a quandary I had never experienced before.

It was 1962, and I had chosen not to work outside the home because of the children. It was winter, cold, and lots of snow, and I was stuck in the house every day, taking care of kids. We were all healthy, and Spencer was working, and though there was not ever enough money or time, things were going well, but I was miserable. It had started two years before, and it only happened in the winter months when I couldn't be out and around. I felt guilty, lost, like something was missing. I would get my Bible out of hiding and read to alleviate the lost feeling.

We were not attending church regularly because my husband worked retail six days a week and felt that Sunday was his day of rest. Reading the Bible would make me feel pretty good while I was doing it, but some hours later, that odd feeling would return. I found myself reading more and more. I was in the book of Galatians, and it didn't make any sense. The letter Paul wrote to the church at Galatia seemed harsh and disturbed me. But I continued on and found myself in the letter to the church in Ephesus, which gave me more comfort, but the feeling of lostness kept creeping in.

I couldn't sleep. I have always hit the pillow and immediately fallen to sleep, but I was tossing and turning while my husband snored. One sleepless night, when the lost feeling was totally enveloping me, I just turned to God and asked Him why He had forsaken me. I felt foolish asking that because it was what Jesus had said on the cross, and I was not in His situation at all. He was the perfect, sinless Son of God taking upon Himself the sin of the world and the judgment of His Father. And I knew I was not perfect. I had been taught that when you received Him as your Savior, He would never leave you nor forsake you, but I felt lost, even though I knew I had received Him as my Savior.

A small voice in my head said, "I have not forsaken you; you have forsaken Me!"

"No," I said, "I haven't. I've been good, a good wife and mother. I have not stolen or killed or committed adultery."

But still, I felt lost, so a few seconds later, I had to say it again: "Why have You forsaken me?" and that small voice repeated again that He hadn't, but I had forsaken Him.

One more time, I asked the same question and received the very same answer. I lay there for a few moments in the dark bedroom, and a light bulb went on in my head, and the thought came to me that I really had forsaken Him. I had not given Him the time of day. I only prayed when one of us was sick or we desperately needed money for bills. I didn't go to church. I didn't give money. I had not had any real interest in Him or what He wanted.

As I considered what my attitude toward my creator had been, I realized that I had just been using God for my own desires. At that point, I agreed with Him, finally, and then I felt that He deserved an inventory of what was important to me, so the conversation continued.

After I asked for forgiveness, a sense of peace came over me, but I felt the need to let Him know that He was going to be higher on my priority list. I had to relinquish my right to lots of things that had been taking first place in my life, so I began my list. I told Him that if He wanted to take my husband's life or health, I would accept it. I had been taught that He is good and does only good for His children, so I could trust Him to only do that which was good for me. I gave him permission to allow me or the kids to be sick or die, and even if He wanted us to live in a poverty-stricken hut, that would be fine, because He is good.

I was at peace and ready to sleep, but one more thought entered my mind: What if God wanted me to have more children? Whoa! God is good and knows that we are at our limits with time, space, and money. He would never expect us to have any more children, but if He did … well, "Sure, Father God, if You want it."

And then I fell into a peaceful sleep. Those lost feelings never returned, but instead of the lost feelings, there developed a hunger to know more about this God who loved me so much that He had been working for the last three years to get my attention.

I found a Christian bookstore downtown and began buying good sound doctrinal books, and after a few little miracles, we started going to church. I was just beginning the journey, the walk of faith in the abundant life He had promised me. Sometime later, after much reading, I had the impression that I needed to understand things from His point of view, even His Word. I did not want to just accept anything that any church or preacher or book had to say as truth. I desperately wanted *the* truth, nothing less, nothing more. It was almost like when Solomon was asked by God what one thing he would ask for and was given wisdom as a gift. I needed to have God's help in the learning process and asked for that. Slowly, I was beginning to learn to use my guide.

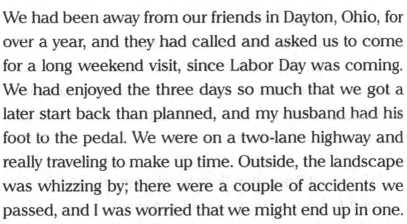

We had been away from our friends in Dayton, Ohio, for over a year, and they had called and asked us to come for a long weekend visit, since Labor Day was coming. We had enjoyed the three days so much that we got a later start back than planned, and my husband had his foot to the pedal. We were on a two-lane highway and really traveling to make up time. Outside, the landscape was whizzing by; there were a couple of accidents we passed, and I was worried that we might end up in one.

I quietly said to Spencer, "Please slow down; we have precious cargo in the car": three kids in the back and one in my lap (no seat belts in the cars then).

He said not a word but pushed down on the accelerator a bit more. I waited a few more minutes before I mentioned again that I thought we were going too fast, and once more, his foot pressed down harder on the pedal. I am sure he just didn't want to hear anything more from me and knew that if I saw that anything I had to say about speeding would just make us go faster, I would shut up.

I did shut up, but in my thoughts, I turned to my Lord and asked Him to help my husband see that he was going too fast, but I didn't want us to end up on a telephone pole for him to learn his lesson, so please work it out.

Within seconds of thinking this prayer to God, a delightful sound came from our rear. It was a state patrol car with a beautiful trooper pulling us over. I said not a word but thank you to the Lord.

When we got home, I said, "I think I am responsible for the ticket, dear," and told him about my prayer.

It made an impression on him, for then he knew that not only did he have me to deal with but the Lord too. And I had learned that I could trust my guide to do the very best thing for all of us.

We were still not attending church regularly, and Sunday seemed to be the worst day of the week. I was feeling guilty because I had been raised going every Sunday, but Spencer did not feel guilty at all. He was thankful he had a day off. He had forgotten a prayer he had prayed years before. He had asked the Lord to give him a job at a store that was closed on Monday so he could get rest and go to church too. God had not forgotten that prayer.

One day, a lady from church came by to visit me and inquired about our not coming to church often; the interesting thing was that the pastor went by to see Spencer at work the same day. Somehow, Spencer remembered that prayer while talking with the pastor, and all of a sudden, it dawned on him that the store that he had been assigned to was closed on Monday mornings. We have never heard of a retail store being closed on Monday mornings since then.

He realized God had answered his prayer, so he came home and told me, "Perhaps we should start going to church on a regular basis."

I then told him about my visit too, and I agreed that now was the time. We did just that and found that our Sundays became much better, even though we had added another project to our family's schedule. Both of us were growing, spiritually.

Some months later, Spencer had another visit at work. This time, it was the man who owned the shoe store next to the clothing store Spencer managed. He was opening a new clothing and shoe store in Wisconsin and wanted Spencer to move there and manage it. Since we were so involved in our church, he told him no, but this man really wanted him. A few months later, he came by the store and asked one more time, and again Spencer said no. When he approached him some weeks later, we decided to pray about it. On faith, Spencer accepted the position of manager of the new store in a growing city in Wisconsin and went there alone, with plans to look for a place for us to live during his off time.

After three months later, no home big enough for our

family of six had turned up, so he drove back to South Bend to pick me up and take me with him to check out a place in Beloit that someone had suggested. Because church had become a real priority to us, we looked in the telephone directory to see if there was a listing for a Southern Baptist church, and we found one. We met with the landlord, and the location was just about perfect; we signed the lease on Sunday.

On Monday, we located the church on a map of Beloit and drove by, not expecting anyone to be there but just wanting to find it so that when we moved, we could go and visit, but there was something going on and people were there. They were having Vacation Bible School.

The pastor's wife met us and after visiting for a while, she shared an envelope where she had written a small prayer while waiting for a doctor's appointment. Her list included "a young couple" to join and work with the church. We looked at each other and had the assurance that God had wanted us in Wisconsin. In July 1965, we moved to the Badger State and joined the church on the first Sunday there. It was a small congregation, and almost every member was a transplanted southerner. I joked that perhaps it was listed as a Southern Baptist church because there were so many members who had moved from the South.

That following spring, I found myself feeling nauseous and had the horrible thought that I might be pregnant. No, God was not going to let this happen again. I did not remember my list where I had given God my permission to have another child, and I got mad at Him. Those first four months found me trying to sleep away reality, but when I felt life stirring, I accepted the fact that we were going to have our fifth child, and it had to be all right, because God only gives good gifts and had a reason for this child to come into the Brown family.

I had been praying for patience, trying to mother the brood we had, and here it came in diapers. I had been expecting patience to arrive in a gift-wrapped package, just all of a sudden, out of the blue, and I would open it and put it on and be patient, but I discovered that my temperament needed the change. It was a process that would include breaking down my natural tendencies and helping me to see my loving God at work, using people and circumstances to make me patient. It would take a longer time than it took to open a package.

Dallas was born five months after Gordon began kindergarten. I had five months of half-days to enjoy the quiet, and when we brought the fifth child home from the hospital, the quiet half-days disappeared. So much work, so little time and energy made me feel I couldn't get it all done to my satisfaction; feeling sorry for myself became my mode of living. My dear husband could see that I was not able to function as before and asked me what burdened me most. He was still in retail and wore shirts and ties every day of the week, and I couldn't keep up with the ironing. It went into the refrigerator in a plastic bag after it was dampened to prevent the clean shirts and hankies from mildewing; there was always a bag in there.

When I mentioned my problem, he suggested I not iron the hankies but fold them right off the line. It was a small thing, but it made the greatest difference in my attitude. There was at least one thing less I had to iron. By following the advice of my God, I could restore my sanity.

We all got involved in church life Sunday mornings and evenings and Wednesday prayer meetings and groups for the kids. One night, we stayed for potluck after the evening's service; it was getting late, and school was waiting for the kids early the next morning. I was helping clean up the fellowship hall with a few others, and the kids were just running around, having fun with their buddies. I had to take charge of the situation, so naturally, I raised my voice to ensure that my commands were heard over the fun, and everyone would get in line.

A few minutes later, the pastor's wife came over to me with a tape recorder in hand and turned it on so I could hear what everyone there had been hearing. The harsh loud voice was mine, and I stood there as it sunk in and made me aware, really aware of what my kids were regularly exposed to as I managed my household. What a good lesson I had that night and how thankful I am for someone caring enough to do a hard thing and risk the loss of a friendship.

Andrew was in the second grade and came home from school one winter afternoon full of excitement; he was pleased with himself, and while taking off the layers of clothing, he told me that he had, all by himself, pushed a buggy into a big snow bank in the parking lot of the grocery store, which was across the street from the elementary school. I wondered why he was so proud of that, as I envisioned a doll buggy, but only said, "Oh, really?" and let it go as I continued making supper, and he didn't offer any more comments.

Dinner was ready when Spencer came home from work, and we were all sitting at the dining table and taking our first few bites after the blessing when the phone rang. I answered because I was closest, and an unfamiliar voice asked me if I had a son named Andrew. I said yes and he went on to tell me that our son had pushed his Volkswagen into a snow bank in the parking lot.

At first, I was startled, and then it dawned on me that the buggy Andrew had been telling me about was a car. I reassured him, after I regained my composure and found out that no damage had been done to the car, that we would definitely take care of disciplining our son. I had a hard time holding back my laughter as I related the story to Spencer and our seven-year old's eyes got wider as he realized that something he thought was trivial was not; somehow, an action he had taken had been found out, and there were consequences he had not expected. We did have a firm talk about respecting other's property to our son. It is a sure thing that our "sins will find us," as scripture says, and it is a good thing that God makes sure we teach our children "the fear of the Lord is the beginning of wisdom" when they are young.

This small incident did make a difference in his life because he grew up knowing that all actions have consequences, and he has been thoughtful and responsible toward God and others. He went on after graduating from high school and put himself through college working summers, laying carpet for a friend of ours and selling vacuum cleaners, while his older brother received a Naval ROTC scholarship and flew helicopters in the navy.

Gordon had a good friend his age and in the same ninth grade class who lived two doors down. His two older brothers were whizzes in school, especially math and sciences, and Gordon had leanings more toward the creative arts. He drew beautifully and loved to put models together. There were all sorts of aircraft displayed in his room—on shelves and even hanging from the ceiling. When his report card started showing that he wasn't working at studying, we investigated and found that his friend wasn't doing too well in school either. He had lost interest in achieving, partly because it was harder work for him than his brothers and partly because his friend encouraged him with more fun times than school work.

We started praying for God to give us something to inspire Gordon to study. Then, an idea came to us, and I am sure it was God who gave it. We had a friend who was a pastor and also flew small airplanes and was involved in the Civil Air Patrol. Jim also gave lessons in flying. We could not afford to give Gordon flying lessons, but we could possibly afford an hour in the air with Jim. Gordon's birthday was coming soon, and we bought one half-hour up in a Piper Cub, with Jim selling math and science skills as a prerequisite to becoming a pilot.

It worked, and Gordon set a goal to fly and became more serious about school. Later, in college, he lost track of book work because he is a hands-on, practical person rather than a theory person. It was an ad on TV about the Army offering an opportunity to fly without a college degree that convinced him to sign up. A few years later, Gordon was in helicopter flight school, and a few years later, he was teaching new pilots how to fly. He served his country well, fighting fires in California and Honduras and delivering and rescuing soldiers in Saudi Arabia and Somalia and patrolling borders in Korea and Germany before he retired after twenty years. He loved flying, and his dad and I have found such satisfaction in knowing that when the Lord tells parents to find what their child is interested in and help direct them to that goal, He promises that they will keep to the path.

It was always fun to learn something new. I could get really excited about the learning process, but following through was another story. Getting to the end of a project was a challenge because another new experience was always ahead and appealed to me more than finishing an old one.

In 1978, my friend Alice asked me to work with her in her cleaning business. I was ready to get out of the house for a few hours a day and get paid to do the thing I regularly did for free. It was just perfect for me at that time, with our youngest in school. I was part of a team going into homes and businesses doing general cleaning. I helped Alice repair equipment and get supplies ready for the next day's work, and later she asked me to keep records and answer the phone and do the scheduling. She was preparing me for the time she would leave, though I didn't know it. When she approached me about buying the business in 1985, I felt I didn't know enough about the commercial end of things, but I finally jumped in, with Spencer's approval. God was ready to teach me a whole lot and, in the process, change me a lot. The responsibility didn't weigh too heavily on me because I had run a home for thirty years, paying bills and shopping and scheduling and cleaning.

I really enjoyed it but found that I wasn't in as much control as I thought I would be. Employees were not as concerned about making the customers happy as I was or even working when they were needed. Customers had a way of finding another company that would do the work better or cheaper. The IRS and insurance companies were very demanding, as were our suppliers. Sometimes, I would wake up in the middle of the night and not be able to get back to sleep for worrying about events that happened. I prayed a lot and waited a lot. God was teaching me that He knew best, even when things went bad. Waiting is really hard for me, since I am impatient, and finishing a difficult job instead of learning a new one was hard to deal with. I had to understand how to finish what I had started, and that would take endurance. That was not a quality I had been endowed with, naturally. It became evident to me that I needed to read the book of directions more. This made me decide to start getting up earlier in the mornings and spending time reading and praying for the things that concerned me. Each morning, I would read one of David's Psalms, and then I started reading a chapter in Proverbs. I began writing my prayers rather than thinking them because I wanted to be very aware of what I was saying and not let sleepiness take over and then I could record answers when God responded.

As I got to know my creator and His ideas and ways, my notion of how big and sovereign He was changed. How I thought about God made all the difference. He really was in control of everything; He really loved His creation, and He had a plan. I could rely on Him, absolutely. He was trustworthy. My fears were needless and were actually denying His love and power. It had been easy to lean on my own understanding when I had little knowledge of the largeness of God and His ways, but now my understanding was being enlightened, and there was God to consider.

I was a rational person, and would never imagine that an employee would take a company vehicle for their own purpose, and in the middle of the night without asking permission first. One night, that actually happened; the young man not only borrowed the car, he ran it into a tree and totaled it.

It struck me that I had been guilty of doing the same things with God's possessions. He was the creator, and everything belonged to Him, rightfully, and I had presumed what I had was mine to do with as I chose. Many times, I foolishly used time and money to please myself.

Then there was the problem of training our workers to use the chemicals and equipment and the protocol. It seemed to go into one ear and out the other when they were out working. They did what they wanted, and sometimes it was not the way they were trained. They ignored the teaching, and I could see myself not paying attention to the direction book or basically disobeying it.

God had been so patient with me over the years and sometimes let me learn the hard way, getting the results of doing it wrong so I would remember the next time to do it His way. This business was a school for me. If I studied the book of directions and cooperated with my guide and did not lean on my own understanding, it would work better, and I would be better too.

Discipline isn't a four-letter word, but the thought of it was as distasteful to me as if it were. I'm talking about having to do essential things when it is necessary and learning that the chore of taking care of the maintenance on the vehicles and equipment should be welcomed and not resented. We sometimes assume that because we are a child of God's and He is taking care of us, that all should run smoothly. We are bound for heaven, but we are not there yet. I needed to learn that when problems came, I must submit under God's hand and go about solving them step-by-step, trusting Him each step of the way. I always learn something new when problems confront me, and when I get through them, I am better prepared for the future when another problem arises. We have been told that we will have tribulations, so we can count on that. But we have also been told that He would be with us till the end. God doesn't humble us, but we must humble ourselves and accept that God is working.

I ask God, "What are you trying to teach me?" and "What do I need to do?" I pray for wisdom to make good decisions and help to see the right path. It is surprising to me how involved the Lord is in my life, in little things and the big ones too. This relationship is developing into more than anything the earth has to offer. God Himself deigns to serve me.

The phone rang about 2:30 on a cold, snowy, and windy night in February 2004, waking me. It was one of our employees telling me that our car had troubles on the interstate and a highway patrolman would not let it sit there. I had to get dressed and drive out to where they were, load all the supplies into my car, and transport the team to their next account. The car had to be towed and repaired later, but the team needed to get their job done.

After I took the team back home, I went to the office a little early to do my work for the day. I had to trust that God was in charge, and though the situation demanded much from me, I got through. He always gives the grace needed for the situation he has allowed to develop in your life. A normal day with all things working is a joy, and I am much more grateful for things working than I used to be. Our country is so blessed with so many good things that we take for granted, like the availability of gas and food and repairmen, that we forget how other people have to live in some parts of the world. It is a small thing to be waked in the middle of a sound sleep to take care of a problem.

Our company had really grown; we were about five times bigger than when we had bought it. We had several good accounts and one especially large one with a number of our employees working it. We had bought lots of equipment to use on these accounts, and of course, the accompanying bills associated with payroll were increasing. One bright September day in 2001, terrorists not only hurt our country, they had drastic effects on our company. Two weeks later, the large account sent us notice that they were quitting our service in thirty days.

For the first time, our workers were unemployed, and claims on our unemployment insurance and lots of bills that had accumulated as we grew still had to be paid. Then there were other accounts that cut back their services; some even moved out of our area. We were losing business for the first time since we began. It got really tight financially. Good employees began leaving the area too, looking for jobs elsewhere. We were not paying ourselves, and we cut our personal insurance to help the company keep going.

It looked bleak and hopeless, but God was still in charge, even though I couldn't see what good was in the whole situation. The guidebook tells us what to think on instead of thinking on the problem or the world system, it tells us to, first of all, think on whatever is good. There were days when I really tried to come up with something good, but nothing would come to mind, so all the good I could think of was God Himself and that is what I focused on: His works, His creation, His love, His Savior.

Even then, I did become discouraged for a while. We had put so much effort into the building of the business, and it seemed to be a wasted effort. I did not want our kids to have to take care of us, as it appeared might happen. One afternoon, I was walking down the hall from my office near the back of our building towards the front door. There was a large set of windows on the front of our building, and the sun would shine directly into my eyes every cloudless afternoon, almost blinding me. I was stewing about my situation, as usual, but there was another light that appeared in the center of my head for just a second. It was like a spark that was bright for just an instant and a knowing that God was going to make it work out. I kept on walking to the front, but I was different because God had touched me and had sparked hope and peace in my being. I wish I could recapture that moment, but all I can do is remember it.

Things didn't change perceptibly for a long while. I still had to play with paying accounts and pray for other hurting companies to pay us. Some things got neglected, like repairing equipment and definitely not buying any new stuff. But about a year later, we got a notice saying that we had to move, and it was the Lord moving us to a cheaper location and one that was closer to many of our customers, which would save gas and driving time for the teams.

Gradually, the vehicles got paid off; insurance was cheaper because we had fewer employees and less room. I determined to pay off all the credit cards we had so liberally used when money was flowing in; I did not want to use them again. I also determined to be more careful about everything. If you are not motivated to do the right thing, God will give you the motivation.

We had a company policy to not advance money before payday to employees and never to loan money to them. Some of our policies were tough, and somehow, my attitude changed because of the dire straits we had been in. I found myself more compassionate and giving than before. I had tried protecting the company from harm, and harm had come anyway, but God was seeing me through, so I could trust Him to provide through me for some needs of our people. Someone would ask for a little cash to tide them over till payday, and I would go to my purse and get out, sometimes, my last dollar and give it to them. It didn't hurt one bit.

The phones weren't ringing off the hook with new customers wanting a bid, but we had stopped hemorrhaging accounts. Gasoline prices were hurting us, and minimum wage increased. I assessed out accounts and raised rates on some and added a mileage surcharge to others to defray some of the expense. A few new accounts were added, and we were getting by. A construction clean-up appeared out of nowhere, and then another one, and we found ourselves, personally, going to these and working too, but there was money coming in. I had started working a nightly account to save on payroll, and Dallas worked with me. Not only did it give me a new insight on the routine of commercial cleaning that our crews have to go through and the problems that arise and how our chemicals and equipment work (or not), but I regularly had opportunities to hear from our son and to have input into his life. I occasionally had thoughts as to why at my age I was doing this, but then I thought, *what else would I be doing at this time of night? I am having hands-on experience.*

It gave me a chance to share hints and suggestions I learned with our workers and let them know how I appreciated them and what they did. I was willing to do what lay before me and trust God to bring the right accounts to us at the right time, and I prayed every day for Him to bless the work of my hands. He is so good, and His timing is perfect, and I say, with confidence, "My life is in His hands."

We made payments on our line of credit, and I also gave raises to employees. We had a balance in our checking account at the end of the month and were able to pay vendors on time.

My mother's mother had moved in with my folks when I was born, to help out, and she stayed (I can only guess that I must have been a handful). She was a big influence on my life as I grew up, partly because she sometimes took my part when she felt I was being picked on, and I really appreciated that. She taught us girls to pray each night before we went to sleep. I have no idea where this prayer originated, but it was religiously quoted every night even when I was a teenager: "Now I lay me down to sleep, I pray, the Lord my soul to keep. If I should die before I wake, I pray the Lord my soul to take." And if we were still awake after those two sentences, we added personal requests. That was the extent of my prayer life for some years. Next to the dresser mirror hung her little plaque, "Prayer Changes Things," and I often looked at it.

One time, I asked my dad why we had to pray about things when God knew about everything anyway. He gave me a good answer: When we asked God for specific requests and He answered them, our faith would grow, and we would have something to thank Him for and also share with other people.

Later, I began thinking that God was sometimes quite demanding in wanting us to pray about everything, and there may have been a little resentment over the way He chose to work. Why did He not just go ahead and take care of problems if He loved me, instead of wanting me to make a request? After all, there were always problems facing me, and sometimes I didn't remember to go to Him in prayer because of the urgency or tendency to dive right in and try to figure it out. I have discovered that when I draw Him into my situation, I have a confidence that I don't have when I don't turn to Him.

Sometimes, the situation is minor, and sometimes, it is difficult, but what He really desires is that we be humble enough to recognize our limitations. Since we don't know everything, as He does, and therefore cannot know all the possibilities, we are short-changing ourselves when we don't use the greatest resource in the whole universe, and we don't have a chance to get to know Him.

When I find myself so concerned that I keep repeating my request, I have to remind myself that my prayer has been sent, like a letter dropped in the mailbox. I had to let go of the letter for it to get sent. If I held onto the envelope, it would never get going, so after it was let go, I should be thanking God for answering and start looking and believing He was working. The more I read the guidebook and understood how involved God is in everything and works everything for good in my life, the more I wanted to wait for His solutions. It has been easier to be patient and try to see His hand working and talk to Him about all sorts of things.

For instance, Lee was trying to repair one of our big, expensive floor machines and called for my help because he wasn't able to reach the part behind the cover. I stood there with my foot on the rotating base and began praying that God would give his fingers eyesight to see where the new part was to be placed. It took a few minutes before Lee gave a victorious whoop. God was at work helping us get the machine up and running again; I told Lee what I had been doing while I was helping him. It showed me, again, that I waste lots of time thinking about what is going on rather than turning my thoughts to the Lord. It was a little thing, but my guide was showing me and Lee that nothing is ever too small or big for God not to be trusted for.

Our daughter Christy was such a delight, so beautiful and precious, and we had fun buying girly things for her. As she got into her teen years, though, she knew more than her mamma, and big tensions developed as she became prissy and bossy and critical. When she was in the eleventh grade, she started dating a boy about two years older than she was, and things got worse. She lost interest in furthering her education when he gave her an engagement ring, and she started her hope chest. She didn't even want to learn how to drive because he would take her everywhere; though she wasn't aware, he was really controlling her. We were concerned and could say nothing to her about what she was doing without tempers flaring. We prayed lots, and one afternoon, a friend came by, and we sat at the dining room table and prayed for her. We kept praying and trusting God to change things.

Shortly after that, Christy graduated and started working to save money so she could move out, but then she found out that he was also dating someone else. It crushed her, but I could see that God was answering our prayers. After she broke up with him, she decided to learn how to drive and used her savings to purchase a car. Guess who had to go with her for her behind-the-wheel training? Me.

We took her car to the cemetery, where there was no traffic and those laid to rest there didn't care what we were doing, backing up and turning and going down all the lanes.

God had engineered the whole thing and was giving me a chance to re-establish a good relationship with my daughter. We were alone and talked about everything and became friends. She found a small apartment and bought some furniture and set up housekeeping, and she began to wait for the Lord to bring the right man into her life, which He did. She met Bruce at a New Year's party at a friend's and came home elated. This was it. He was perfect for her, and when we met him, I agreed, but her dad had reservations. Dads and daughters: It is a very protective position.

There was one little problem: He was Catholic. He told Christy that he had become a Christian while at college, and she seemed to trust that was true. We were taking the *Moody Monthly Magazine*, and it just happened that the latest issue had a big article titled "Can a Catholic Be a Christian?" I was reading it when Bruce came to take Christy out on a date. I casually laid the opened magazine on the arm of the sofa and excused myself to go do something, all the while praying that he would notice the title and perhaps read the article.

A few minutes after leaving the room, I heard a very loud "What the ...!" and the sound of a magazine being thrown across the room.

I gathered that Bruce had seen the article. I don't remember that we had a deep conversation before the two left the house, but before he asked for Christy's hand and gave her an engagement ring, we were assured that he was a true believer in Jesus, the Christ.

They were married that following August and moved to Dallas, where his firm transferred him. They were going to be very neutral when it came to finding a church and visited several nondenominational ones. One Saturday, they were sightseeing in downtown Dallas and drove by the First Baptist Church. Bruce saw the marquee announcing the topic of Dr. Criswell's message the next day. It was to be on Revelation; Bruce had a deep interest in that book, and they decided to visit. Just a few weeks later, Bruce asked to be baptized into their membership, and the service normally held on a Sunday evening was changed to the morning so Bruce could share his declaration of belief with the whole television audience in addition to the congregation.

As I have been involved in this journey, I have learned to expect tests along the way, as God has promised. I have come to understand that this test is not to let God know how we are progressing, for He knows everything from beginning to the end, but to let us identify the flaws in our character, faith, or understanding of His guidebook. Anything worth its value has to be tested: airplanes to be sure they fly safely, furnaces to be sure they won't blow up, and washing machines and on and on. We trust that the makers of the items we buy are selling us stuff that works, that it has integrity. God has to make sure that we know what needs working on and to be willing to proceed as He works everything to conform us to the image of our older brother, Jesus. Everything that comes into our lives is filtered through God's hand, so that only what will work to that end will accomplish His great purpose. I used to hate the tests until I understood how much God loves me; He will not allow me to be tested beyond what I can endure. The grace to get through will be there when I need it.

Spencer and I had been married almost twenty-five years, and I was frustrated with my husband. Granted, he worked six days a week and long days too, but I felt that he wasn't carrying his fair share of the load. I had tried talking to him about this problem, and his solution was for me to make lists for him to do. If something happened that needed immediate input from him but it wasn't on the list, he would not think to do it. I wanted him to care enough to see and do without my making a list. Several times I had asked him to go out for coffee where we could talk over a table in a public place and the parameters would limit our emotions. He would seem to understand what I was trying to get at and agree with me over the cups, but his behavior would not change at home. It had reached the limit when our church was remodeling, and he was more than willing to go there every night, after his dinner, and help do things he never had time for at home.

I was finished with trying to communicate. I was smoldering. One day, as I was ironing in the basement (which had not been a project of his and needed so much work), I decided that I was going home to my mother and stay for a while. I would leave him with the children and the work and let him really see, firsthand, what I saw every day. I finished ironing and fixed dinner, and when he came through the front door, I was ready to tell him what I was going to do, when he grabbed me by the hand and marched me into our bedroom without a word.

He then told me that God had spoken to him on his thirty-minute drive from work, and we needed to talk. I was astonished. He wanted to talk.

We sat on the bed, and he confessed how blind he had been and was definitely going to make more of an effort to do his part. I was in tears before he finished and realized that even though I had been so angry and feeling sorry for myself and had not prayed about my decision to leave, God had intervened. Things did gradually get better, and I not only knew that God loved me and was concerned about me, I also knew that my husband loved me a lot.

It is a funny thing, in an interesting way, what attitudes develop in kids who are raised attending Sunday school and church on a regular basis. My folks were as serious about my going to church as they were about me going to school, and only a high fever or a broken back or something of that nature was to keep me from either place. Over the years, I am sure I heard the entire Bible preached or taught, and I memorized many passages and verses.

We had a thing called a "Sword" drill, since the Bible refers to itself as the "sword of the Word of God." It was a competition, and we kids would line up next to each other, holding our identical Bibles. The referee would call out a verse without giving its location, and at "Go," we would draw our "swords," opening the Bible and looking for that verse. The first one to find it took a step forward. I was good at it and competed in our statewide competition.

I knew a lot about the Bible and Old Testament stories about Daniel in the lion's den; Shadrack, Meshack, and Abednego; Samson; and David. But it was only when I started attending a women's Bible study at the age of thirty-six that I discovered the man Jesus. We all used the New Testament Good News for Modern Man, and the guide would read comments, and we looked up verses and answered prepared questions and then shared our answers with each other. Over the twelve weeks of going through the Gospel of Mark, I got to see up close the thoughts and words and actions of the God-Man who came to earth and lived a perfect life for thirty-three years.

What an impression it made on me, a girl who had been exposed to so much Bible as a child. I fell in love with Jesus during this small group study, which was something that had not happened earlier.

Not only did I fall in love with Jesus, but I was brought to the point with the questions and comments by the guide of applying what I learned, and I believe that was what made another big difference in my life. My relationship with Him had a real footing because I had some knowledge of Him that was real and personal, and I could interact with Him in a real and personal way, based on facts.

All the knowledge of the Bible I had been taught had not given me much more than pride prior to this awakening of my love for the author. But all this knowledge, since then, has been a strong foundation to build my faith on, and I am most grateful for my parents making sure I went to all the classes and services.

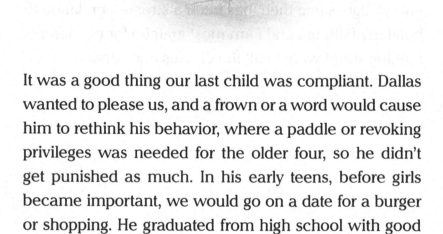

It was a good thing our last child was compliant. Dallas wanted to please us, and a frown or a word would cause him to rethink his behavior, where a paddle or revoking privileges was needed for the older four, so he didn't get punished as much. In his early teens, before girls became important, we would go on a date for a burger or shopping. He graduated from high school with good grades and a desire to get into foreign relations. He was good in Spanish and communicated well. So, college it was.

He was attending the University of Maryland, a faraway place, but since his older brother lived in Maryland and my sister lived in Virginia, I didn't worry too much. He was naturally charming and tall and slender; he looked so much like his father did at twenty-two. He had found this wonderful part-time job at a big corporation in the corporate offices and also was working at a department store part-time. All seemed to be going good for him. He had come home in June on a week's break, and his dad had gone over his bills with him. He had promised to work at his job the weekend after he got back to Maryland and save his money.

That weekend was the Fourth of July, 1989, and Dallas's fraternity roommate pressured him to go to the 4th bash at Ocean City that all students went to. Dallas made his decision to go have fun instead of working and left the corporate offices after putting in his hours. It is a six-hour drive to Ocean City, so he must have arrived at Johnnie's, the meeting place, close to midnight, Friday, June 30.

Meanwhile, in Wisconsin, I was planning my own weekend. Saturday, I was going to clean house and go to the grocery store. Sunday was church, as usual, and some rest for Monday to get payroll to the point of cutting checks on Wednesday, payday. Tuesday, I would catch up on the ironing. It had been a warm, calm Sunday, and I was watching TV in the bedroom and napping a bit before actually getting in bed. Spencer was in the family room, doing the same (we have different taste in some programs). The phone rang about eleven o'clock, and though it was late, I was not too concerned because employees do call all hours to say they can't work, and Monday was the day before the holiday, and it could be a long weekend for someone.

I prepared myself for an excuse, but I wasn't prepared for the call—from Maryland. The woman introduced herself as the aunt of Dallas's roommate, Gerald, and wanted me to know that Dallas was in the hospital in Maryland. Her voice was controlled and quiet as she spoke of the accident. It was Gerald's car, and Gerald's wallet that had been found; it was first thought that it was Gerald who was driving. They did look quite a bit alike, and she had been notified by the authorities. She had even been to the hospital and thought it was Gerald in the bed in a coma, until he called and expressed concern because Dallas hadn't returned with his car yet.

It seemed that Dallas, being the gentleman that he always is, had volunteered to take a young lady home about 4 a.m. when her boyfriend didn't want to leave. Gerald suggested he take his car because it was parked much closer than Dallas's. He always put his wallet under the driver's seat for safekeeping when he went out. Only then did she know it was Dallas laying in the hospital bed with a fractured arm and in a semi-coma. He had been extracted from the wreck with the jaws-of-life and helicoptered to the hospital Saturday morning about 5:30.

When she said, "He is all right," I said, "All right?" In a semi-coma didn't seem all right to me.

I felt the beginnings of a cold sweat develop on my forehead. I leaned against the chest of drawers and tried to realize that this was a real call about my son. Fear which I had not felt before was there with me, and I had to force myself to not faint. Then, Spencer appeared in the hall, being curious about the late phone call. He was only hearing my end of the conversation but was gathering the news. I heard him in the bathroom, throwing up. It is funny how people react to awful news. I felt faint, and he felt sick.

I picked up a pencil and wrote down the name of the hospital, the phone number, and the city. As I was taking notes, I had the immediate confidence that God was involved in this happening, and while I had spent my Saturday and Sunday in a most normal way, knowing nothing about my son's predicament, God had been taking care of Dallas for two days already. Somehow, I had a sense of peace, realizing that God is never surprised and always provides grace for all our surprises.

After telling Spencer all I had learned, I immediately called the hospital and was connected to the intensive care unit and asked about Dallas, who had been admitted as Gerald. I was reassured by a kind and professional nurse that his life signs were stable, and yes, he was still in a semi-comatose state. She added how glad she was that this young man had a mother. I told her that I would be there as soon as I could get there and asked her to please continue taking good care of Dallas.

As I hung up, I turned to Spencer and the first thing I said was, "God is involved in this; there are too many out of the ordinary happenings."

I knew God had a plan and was working it out, and I had better get into His flow and trust Him totally. This was something completely out of my hands. I felt that I was being carried along on a journey not of my choosing. I picked up the phone again, and even though it was midnight, I started calling our kids. They needed to be praying, and their churches needed to be praying too. After the last call, we started planning how to get me to Maryland, and the phone rang again. It was Evan, Dallas's third roommate, to tell us that Gerald couldn't talk because he was so broken up over what had happened and to ask what he could do. I asked him to notify Dallas's pastor and told him to pray.

Then I headed for the ironing board. I had to think and pray, and what better place to do that than the ironing board? Besides, I couldn't sleep or sit, and the ironing needed to be done. Then I started packing. I got to bed about 4:00 and the alarm was set for 5:15, but I was up and dressed by then. I had to finish payroll and call my sister in Virginia and the travel agent. Fortunately, Dorothy was home, and yes, she and her husband would pick me up at Washington's International Airport and even take me to hospital.

I managed to get tickets and then called Dot to let her know what time to expect me. I called the intensive care unit again, and the nurse told me that Dallas was about the same. I was grateful that I had so much work to do that I didn't have time to think and imagine the car crashing into Dallas and the pain he was in. I had no time to worry. Somehow, the checks got done, ready to hand out on Wednesday, and we hurried to O'Hare Airport. The ticket was discounted because it was a day before a holiday, and the earliest flight was to leave O'Hare at 12:30. On the plane, I would not allow myself to picture what Dallas had been through or even what he was going through now. I had worked in hospitals and seen people come in after an accident. To venture too close in my thoughts gave me the feeling that I'd cave in, so I tried reading and praying.

We had been so fortunate raising our five children with no disasters happening like so many people encounter that I did not wonder why this happened to us. Occasionally, I might have questioned why bad things had *not* happened. We were not immune. But I never questioned after the phone call some basic things that I have built my life on:

1) that God is good,
2) that God is sovereign,
3) that I was His child by grace through faith in Jesus's payment,
4) that He never gave His children more than they could bear,
5) that I'd given Him permission to do as He wanted in my life a long time ago, and
6) that He causes all things to work together for good to those who love Him and are called according to His purpose. There was a real peace in my heart as I traveled to be with Dallas.

The International Airport looked the same as it had when we lived there thirty years before, but really, really busy. I strained looking for Dot and Dwayne's faces among all the strangers, and tears came to my eyes when I found them in the crowd. She gave me a big compassionate hug while Dwayne found my luggage, and then we were in the car, heading for the hospital, six hours away. Of course, we got lost trying to find the right exit, and I had to remember to be patient. It was a hot July in DC, and the air conditioner was on full blast, so we couldn't talk. That was a good thing for me, as I couldn't make conversation. It was 2:30 when we landed, and I just wanted to be next to Dallas; we seemed to be moving so slowly, and the day was speeding by. Dwayne was hungry about five o'clock, rightly so, and we stopped at a Dairy Queen in a small town. I was not hungry at all and did not want to wait even for fast food. I got a coke.

The road narrowed to a two-laner, and traffic was heavy. It was the third of July; the next day was America's birthday, and her citizens were out to celebrate. Soon, we saw the first sign that mentioned Queensbury. We were getting close. It was seven o'clock and still light out, and we started hunting for the hospital. I was getting nervous. I felt such a sense of relief when I saw a big modern hospital. Even though the city was small, the hospital looked very capable of taking care of all sorts of needs.

Dwayne found parking, and I tried very hard not to rush, but my youngest child was somewhere in that building, and I kept feeling that I needed to be there to touch, pat, kiss, hug, and talk to him.

We found where the intensive care was located; it was now 7:30, and I had been trying to get to Dallas since I left Wisconsin at eleven that morning, which seemed like days ago. We looked at the closed doors on which were printed a large sign with visiting hours: 10, 2, 6, and 10, and 10-15 minutes allowed per visit.

I knocked, and a nurse appeared in scrub gown. "I'm Dallas's mom. Remember the young man called Gerald for two days?"

She smiled and said she was so glad Dallas had a mom. I had heard that before, on the phone last night. And she led me to his bed, which was almost directly across from the double doors. There were two rows of beds with curtains to pull for privacy. Some were pulled, and I glanced around and noted that each exposed bed had monitors and all sorts of serious-looking equipment next to each patient. The room was full of busy nurses helping the thirteen or fourteen patients there.

And there was Dallas. He, too, had appliances attached to him, but he looked so good to me. His head appeared much larger than normal, and his eyes were swollen shut and many shades of purple. There was a cut and a few stitches on his nose, and another cut under his chin. His right arm was in a splint, and he was tied to the bed in poesy. There was a heart monitor attached to his chest and a screen on the wall with the moving dashes, an IV in his arm, a tube in his nose for nourishment, and a catheter with its pouch under the bed.

I leaned over the protective rails and kissed him on his forehead, but there was no response at all. I spoke to him and touched him. It was so good to be there touching him, even though he gave no indication he knew. How ignorant I was about traumatic brain injury.

Dot wanted to see him too, and both of us cried together, so thankful that he was alive. We weren't allowed to stay long, and Dot and Dwayne needed to start for home. I had to go to admitting and correct all the misinformation attached to him. I did not know his Social Security number, but we figured out a way to find it the next day. I sure did not feel like going over all the red tape, but it was a necessary thing. It was about ten o'clock, and I hurried back to the elevator to get to the fourth floor, where a large crowd was gathering around the double doors. It was time again for entry to that busy room where loved ones were being cared for.

As Dot and I got closer to the doors, we saw four people who seemed interested in us. It was Gerald and his aunt, who had called us that night, and her husband and Evan. I do not remember the small talk, but there were condolences and a shared anxiety over Dallas, and at least everyone was in their proper place: Dallas was Dallas in the intensive care unit, and Gerald was Gerald standing in the waiting room, and Barbara Anne was Gerald's aunt, and I was Dallas's mom.

Barbara Anne was concerned about the future and pressed me about what Dallas was going to do: continue to share the apartment with her nephew and continue school at the university or move back home. There was the rent that needed to be paid if he was to stay and live with Gerald and Evan. I did not know what to answer. I did not know what was going to happen. I did not want to disrupt Dallas's life, but how long would his recovery take and would he be able to continue as he had been were the concerns I was having.

She was really concerned with the rent he owed and volunteered to pay his share and he could pay her back, later. I agreed, but I had negative feelings because I had not even seen the doctor and was sticking Dallas out on a limb. She wasn't willing to wait for the answer. Once that question was answered to her satisfaction, everyone began leaving, and it was time for the last visit of the day for the intensive care patients. I walked through the swinging doors towards Dallas's bed, and Dot came with me. She wanted to see him before they left for the long drive back home. We hugged good-bye, and I was most thankful for a wonderful sister and brother-in-law. We made quick plans for meeting on Wednesday and spending the night so we would have time to look for Dallas's wallet and his car and car keys.

Then I turned back to his bed and began to try to wake him up. The nurse had told me that patients in a semi-coma needed lots of stimulation, lots of talking to and attention, and the sooner he woke up, the better for his brain. I was given fifteen minutes four times a day to accomplish this. I didn't want to be too loud because there were some very seriously injured patients there, and I didn't want to disturb them, but I wanted to wake Dallas. The nurses were so gracious to give me a few minutes longer, and I started talking. I reminded him of his brothers and sister and dog and called all their names. No response. I told stories. No response. I touched his forehead and rubbed his shoulders and held his hand. No response.

It was going on thirty minutes, and I suddenly felt bushed, so I gave up for the night. I thanked the nurses and headed out those swinging doors and went down the hall to the elevator to go down to the first floor and catch another elevator to rooms that had been set aside for out-of-town relatives. The cost was minimal and so convenient to be close for the four times a day visits. It was to be my home for the next ten days, and I welcomed it.

When I got to my room, the temperature was 98 degrees, and after a call, the maintenance man came to fix the thermostat while I waited in the lounge area. There was a security guard taking a break watching TV. He was friendly and asked me who I had in the hospital. After I shared a few details, he told me that he, too, had been in auto accident when he was Dallas's age and he, too, had a TBI and went on to tell me of some of his experiences with recovery. I was beginning to find out about head injuries.

I sat, amazed at how God was arranging circumstances to introduce me to someone who could give me insight as to what to expect. We sat and talked while the thermostat was being replaced, and my gratitude to the creator of the universe grew as I realized how He loved me and had planned ahead of time to have the thermostat go bad and the security guard sitting right there to give me needed information and hope. I fell into bed in the comfortable room and went to sleep after saying my prayers. It was almost Tuesday. Then it was Tuesday, and I was up early and eager to meet the challenge of waking my son up from the coma. I had thought ahead and prepared for the sitting and waiting I knew would take place by bringing some knitting. I found the restaurant, but they were not opened, so I went on up to the fourth floor and got the needles and yarn and instructions for the sweater and tried to keep my hands and mind busy till I was allowed entry behind those big double doors again. Others were waiting too, and even though we were strangers to one another, we knew the same thoughts and concerns. A woman about my age was sitting on the sofa next to me and told me about her son who had been hurt at a stock car race on Sunday. He was a spectator standing at the fence when a car flipped over the rail and landed on him. He was very seriously injured with many internal injuries.

We were all horror stricken, but it was somewhat

comforting to know that we were not alone in our pain. So, we all waited, but there were more and more coming in, and I realized that it was the Fourth of July, and holidays mean accidents.

Ten o'clock came, and the nurse arrived and opened the door, and one at a time, we were allowed in. Dallas had had his bath and morning checkup by the nurse and doctor, who I hadn't yet met. I stood close by his bed and started talking. It is hard to try to carry on a conversation with someone who is sleeping. Again, no response, but I kept at it and kept touching him. He seemed even deeper in sleep that the night before; the nurse could see my frustration and came over to let me know that he might be tired from all the paces they had put him through earlier. I left disappointed but relieved, knowing that he could just be tired.

There were lots of calls to make and people to see in insurance and admitting. Friends from Dallas's job called, and a friend from our church back home called to express concern. It was comforting to know that so many people stood by Dallas in their prayers and thoughts. There were some definite concerns that needed God's attention, like Dallas's missing wallet and the keys to his car and where the car was.

I kept reminding myself that God knew about this whole situation before it had happened, and He would help us as we depended on Him.

After a small lunch, I was back in the ICU waiting room with my knitting. Around two o'clock, he became very agitated, and as I would speak, he would turn his head the other way, as though trying to avoid the disturbance. I kept moving from side to side but made no progress in waking him. It was time for knitting this sweater I would probably never wear as I wait for the 6:00 visit. More calls to home and sister and a final stop at insurance. Dallas's job had wonderful insurance, and they even provided a registered nurse to counsel through the medical needs he might have.

I was making many trips up and down elevators and was alone most of the time, so this became my up-and-down prayer room. It was a marvelous place to pray aloud, and I found that my hands automatically reached upward as a child would reach for their father's hand, and I talked to my heavenly Father God in earnest about the son he had given me. I praised Him for all the good I could think of and for His loving kindness.

I pled my case, trusting His best judgment. After the five visits I had been allowed and having no positive results, it dawned on me that if Dallas was going to wake up, it was going to have to be from the inside out, rather than from the outside in. I began praying for the Lord to speak to Dallas's spirit. Dallas had believed that Jesus was his Savior at the age of five, and I knew that if he really was a child of God's, His Spirit had taken up residence in Dallas' spirit, as His Word promises, and He could very easily speak to him in his spirit. I asked for this and thanked God for doing it. The 6:00 visit was no more successful than any other, but by this time, everyone in the ICU knew the names of all our family and friends because I repeated them so often, hoping something would trigger his mind.

I finally quit for that session and went back to my knitting. The panel I was making was getting bigger. Time went slowly by, and once again, it was 10:00 p.m. There was a strong determination in me as I walked to his bedside. Thirty minutes into this session, and I was tiring when a second shift nurse came and stood by me. They were allowing extra time because they knew how important it was for him to wake out of the coma.

This nurse was a young, attractive lady with a voice that was clear like a bell. "Dallas, your mom is here. Wake up and talk to her," she said loudly.

Then I spoke to him, and we were on both sides of his bed so he wasn't able to avoid the noise. We tickled him and stuck our fingers in his ears and blew in his face and rubbed his hands and generally bothered him. He moved around in his bed like he was irritated at the interference, but his eyes kept closed. We kept it up for nearly forty minutes. The nurse let the rail down, and I was able to move closer. She had to get back to her other patients, so I was left alone again and had to move from one side of the bed to the other, as Dallas kept turning his head away from me.

As I was at the foot of his bed on another trip around, he just seemed so disgruntled with me, and I asked him, "Am I bothering you, Dallas? If so, just say 'yes' and I'll quit." And I kept walking to the other side.

"Yes, yes, yes" came out of his mouth.

I stopped my walk and looked at the nurse's station and caught the eye of the one who had been helping me. I asked if she had heard what I thought I had heard. She nodded she had. He had actually heard me and responded. I had to say hallelujah right then, but I had lied to Dallas. I had to keep pestering him even though I had promised I would quit, but to no avail. He had said all he was going to say that night.

It was way past time for me to leave, so with a kiss on his forehead, I bid him good night and went on my elevator rides with a victorious song and a big thank you to the Lord. When I arrived at my quarters, the maintenance man was there again watching TV and encouraged me more after I told him of Dallas yesses. I could hardly wait to call home with the good news. After talking with Spencer and saying quite a long prayer of thanksgiving, I went to sleep looking forward to Dot's visit the next morning. Suddenly, I was wakened by the phone ringing.

After a groggy hello, a deep voice identified himself: "Mrs. Brown, this is Officer Matt Williams."

The grogginess left fast. "Yes, can I help you?" I asked.

"Dallas is in serious trouble. We are not finished with

the investigation into the accident, but from what I gather now, it was his fault, and there will be seven or eight charges against him."

Another fear entered my heart and some anger too. This man woke me near midnight and didn't even have the courtesy to inquire how Dallas was. I tried to hold my words back as I asked questions to find out as much about the accident as I could. He asked me if he could see me the next morning, and I agreed. Now I had something else to look forward to that wasn't as pleasing as being with my sister. Sleep seemed no option, as I had something else to talk to the Lord about.

Wednesday morning broke cloudless and hot again. After a shower and dressing, I headed down the elevator without my knitting and not looking forward to meeting Officer Williams. Dot arrived all the way from Virginia, and I caught her up on all that had happened with Dallas the night before and the phone call. Officer Williams was late, but in full uniform, spit and polished. He was all business and had not changed his approach from the night before. Brusquely, he said again that Dallas was in big trouble with the state of Maryland, and seven or eight charges were being filed against him. He showed me his little notebook with each item listed and the computer printout of Dallas's record. After looking at his papers, I bravely defended my son, who had just hours before managed to get three miraculous yesses out of his mouth. I told him that Dallas wasn't a bad person, that he had made bad judgments with regards to driving, but that he was a child of God's and that God was more than able to discipline him for change. If he needs to change, then, perhaps this was the best way to teach him, and I trust that God will allow only what is best for Dallas.

Again, I was glad that Dot was there for support. Officer Williams left us with the impression that there may even be a warrant out for Dallas's arrest if I were to take him out of the state. What a way to start out the day.

We headed for Dot's car on our scavenger hunt for a car and keys and wallet. The officer had informed us where the wrecker had taken Gerald's car, and that was the first place we were going to search. Barbara Anne had given us the name of the restaurant in Ocean City where the boys had met and guessed that was where Dallas's car was. We decided to look for Gerald's wrecked car and see if Dallas's wallet might be there.

After a few wrong turns, we pulled in to the junkyard and found our way to the office, where we were pointed to the general direction of the wrinkled white auto Dallas had been driving. As we got closer, we could see Dallas's jeans lying on the seat where they had been cut off him, bloody, amongst the many bits of glass. Again, I had to make myself not visualize what had happened to my son. I quickly moved things, looking for keys and a wallet. The top of the car had been cut and bent up in order to extricate the driver, and the front tire was only five inches from the driver's seat. I wondered how anyone managed to come out of that wreck alive. We found nothing but finished searching with lots of small cuts from all the broken glass, even though Dot had thoughtfully brought leather gloves for protection.

We went back to the office and questioned the owner and found out that the paramedics had been on the scene within twenty minutes of the accident; Dallas had been flown by helicopter to the hospital a few minutes after that. He told us exactly where the accident happened and how to get there. It was getting hotter, and we were getting wilted, but we continued our search. In no time, we found the winding road, and then I saw the black skid marks. We turned around, pulled off the road, and started looking around, searching. There were pieces of metal and plastic and broken glass all over the area. It appeared that the S curve where the accident happened had very tall grass, which may have prevented Dallas from seeing oncoming traffic. He was heading east and it was almost daybreak, and perhaps the sun was horizontal to him and maybe blinded him. He could have yawned or sneezed or fallen asleep and driven on the dirt on the first part of the curve and was startled awake by the sound and tried to correct his direction, but was across the center line and heading for the larger vehicle too late to avoid the collision. Perhaps he had put his arm up to protect himself and his head hit it, crunching his forearm against the steering wheel.

I kept looking in the dirt and gravel and grass, and

then I saw the keys to his car just lying in the dust, only a few inches from the asphalt. I could hardly believe it and gave a big yell to Dot as I reach down to grab them. It seemed as though God had just put them there for me to find and kept them safely there from Saturday morning till Wednesday afternoon. It was another wonderful display of God's grace, and we just hugged one another and praised Him. Now, where was the car that the keys belonged to?

We continued eastward to Ocean City, a strip of sand, mostly beach with lots of hotels and restaurants and gas stations and shops. We drove up the strip and tried to catch the names of all the places we passed on both sides of the street. There was no "Johnnie's Place," as Barbara Anne had said. We turned around and drove back the other way. No luck again, so we turned around one more time and drove slower and looked harder. I was growing nervous but was drawn to a building with parking on all sides and partially hidden by nice full evergreens. Then I saw the large sign on top: "Johnathan's." Dot was going to pass, but I urged her to pull in; we drove around the big parking lot, and there was Dallas's little car parked, almost hidden completely by the shrubs. Another praise the Lord came from my lips as we pulled up next to it. I tried the key, and it worked, and then we were able to look into all the hiding places for his wallet. It is forever lost, but we had the car and the key. Now we could eat, and as we gobbled down a pizza, we reflected on our treasure hunt. We had a strange map of signs and marks we hardly understood and just followed and found what we were looking for, with the Lord's help.

We drove back to Queensbury follow-the-leader style, Dot in her car and me in Dallas's car. It was close to 5:00 when we got back. I had missed talking to Dallas at the 10:00 and 2:00 times, but we had accomplished a lot, and it was important stuff. We both looked forward to the next visit in ICU.

Dallas's face was beginning to look more normal. The swelling was down some, though the coloring of his skin was yellowish, as though he was under some strange light. We each took one side of his bed and talked to him. His eyes were still shut, matted lashes knit together. We told him about our day and successful hunt and hoped there would be a response. Some sounds came out of his mouth, like he had heard and was trying to communicate, but it was not intelligible. Too soon, the time was up, and we both made the trek down the praying room and across to the other praying room up to my sleeping room. No dinner was needed as we waited for the next visit time, so Dot suggested we pray. The room was quiet as we each voiced out concerns to our heavenly Father and praised Him for all the large and small miracles given and for the guidance and for the progress in Dallas's recovery. We were very tired after the 10:00 visit and fell asleep quickly. The nurse had told us that Dallas would be moved to a regular room on the orthopedic floor on Thursday. He would soon have surgery to set his right arm, and the doctor and neurosurgeon wanted to see me.

Thursday came bright and hot, and Dot was on her way early to beat the awful traffic heading to Virginia. I headed back to ICU to wait for the doctor and to see Dallas. Clock watching didn't move time any faster, and knitting didn't either, but time finally came for the doors to be opened again. The doctor was standing by Dallas's bed, chart in one hand and a steel instrument in the other, checking reflexes. He then informed me that I would need to make plans for Dallas after leaving the hospital. My son had a traumatic enclosed brain injury, and they did not know the extent of the injury. They had done a CAT scan several hours after he had come in and had since done another. They had found some bruising on the left temporal lobe and front temporal lobe; he would need some rehabilitation after he left the hospital. If he was fortunate, he would be able to walk and move about on his own.

There was some damage to the part of his brain that controlled short-term memory and words. They had also given him medication to prevent seizures and reduce the swelling; they almost had to drill holes in his skull to drain fluid that was accumulating, but the drugs were working, and there was no need to drill. Thank God.

I was having a hard time adjusting to all this information. I was on another journey into head injuries and needed to learn lots. The doctor went on to tell me that his surgery was scheduled to repair his arm as soon as it was safe to put him under anesthesia. They were going to take part of his hip bone and put his arm back together, using plates and screws. The orthopedic surgeon would be talking to me about all that.

The good news was that Dallas was being transferred to a regular room with regular visiting hours; I could see him more frequently and for longer periods of time. I wondered if I had neglected giving him tender words and touches when he was a baby and wanted to give that now. Time to spend with him was even more precious. The room he was given was a double; his roommate was an older gentleman, hard of hearing, so communication was to be negligible with him.

I had found Dallas's watch in the glove compartment of his car and his tennis shoes and camera in the trunk. These could bring back some memories. He arrived still in the poesy with an IV still in his arm and was installed into his bed, rails up. A tray of real food arrived, but it was Cream-of-Wheat and Jell-O and ice cream. He never liked Cream-of-Wheat as a kid, and I knew that wasn't going to go down. He wanted to feed himself, not have his mother feed him, and he only took a few bites. He was sleepy, and I sat in the big green vinyl chair, patiently waiting for him to wake. But it was definitely better than waiting for him than outside the swinging doors in ICU.

A nurse came in and told me that the next day he

was scheduled for physical therapy and more x-rays, and probably Monday they would do the surgery on his arm. His older brother, Jeremy, called to let me know that he and his wife would be coming on Saturday. I knew that would be a very good thing for Dallas and me too. I had lots of news to share with him.

Then, he woke up; he looked at me and said, "Hi, Mom."

It was so casual and so normal and so wonderful. I had longed to hear those two little words. I moved over to him and asked if he knew where he was. He looked all around but couldn't name the place. I told him that he was in a hospital and that he had been in a car accident in Gerald's car. It did not register with him. I had not thought about bringing pictures with me of the family and only had a few in my billfold, but I went to my purse and started showing him a family portrait that had been made when he was about twelve.

I pointed to his sister and asked him who that was, and he said, "Eleven, twenty-two," as if he were saying "Christy." I couldn't help but giggle because he was seriously thinking he said "Christy." Funny thing, he could recite the books of the Bible perfectly, something he had memorized when he was a kid, but lots of words just would come to his mind. I kept talking about his family and dog, but his attention span was short, and he was sleepy again. This was a part of head injuries I found out about later, but I used this time to go to the laundromat across the street to do a small load of laundry for me and to talk with the counselor representing his insurance. She made plans to send him to a rehabilitation center in Baltimore that specialized in TBI as soon as the doctors released him.

Thursday was full of therapy and x-rays, but we had time to tour the hospital with me pushing his wheelchair. He was able to walk on his own, they found out from tests, which proved the brain injury had little effect physically. Friday freed us to expand our travels to the outside, and Saturday brought his friends Evan and Gerald for a visit.

Evan almost cried when he saw the extent of the injuries, but Dallas didn't notice. Then Jeremy and Amy came, and we all just talked and talked and enjoyed each other. Before they left, we made plans for me to leave after Dallas's recovery from surgery when the ambulance would pick him up to transport him to Baltimore. I could leave Dallas's car in their drive, and Jeremy would drop me off at the airport.

On Monday while Dallas was in surgery, I met a nice lady from Wisconsin who worked in the Social Service Department of the hospital. She offered to find the records of the paramedics who brought Dallas in from the accident. She noted the information entered regarding them having to cut the seat belt to remove him and the chemistry lab tests which showed his blood alcohol to be much lower than the legal limit for Maryland. One of the charges Officer Williams had said was against Dallas was not wearing a seat belt. So, Officer Williams did not have his facts straight. This information relieved me of some of the concerns Dallas would have to face later.

The surgery took a long time, but the doctor was happy with what had been accomplished. Dallas mentioned that he had pain in his hip area, where they had taken bone to restructure his arm, and pain where his arm had been worked on; he began to realize that his head had been seriously injured in the accident, but there was no pain there. It puzzled him.

After several checkups and more physical therapy the next day, the doctors finally released him to go to rehabilitation. He would be traveling in the ambulance alone; saying good-bye to him was very hard. I told him that either his dad or I would be visiting him soon and watched as he rode away. Then I went back up the elevator the last time to my room to gather my belongings and head to Jeremy's house in Waldorf in Dallas's little car. The same name, the same face, but a different person in so many ways got on the airplane back to Wisconsin. I had been tenderized considerably by the last ten days. I had experienced a vulnerability that left me wincing at the least felt slight by anyone, and I endured the anguish of hurting for my child and facing a dark unknown for his future. I just had to focus on the next step and the next and the next.

The next Wednesday, when I went to prayer meeting

at church, the pastor welcomed me back and asked how I was doing.

All I could say was, "God is good." If I went into detail of all I had gone through and what Dallas had gone through, it would take way too long, and there would be more questions and answers that I would have to think about, and I just wasn't ready to go through that. All I knew was that God was good, no matter what.

I got back to work in time for the next payroll and with less time to dwell on the state of affairs with Dallas.

We decided that Spencer needed to be the one to visit Dallas the next time. He also sat in with all the doctors working with our son. They were exposing him to computer games and testing and therapies involving working with his hands. They gave him money to go on bus rides to see if he could find his way and money to go grocery shopping for a few items to make a meal and then cook it. He was making good progress, but they cautioned Spencer that he would reach a peak and then progress would taper off; the first days were most important.

Dallas stayed there almost six weeks and then decided he didn't want to be there any longer. When the facility to compare oneself against oneself had been damaged, progress is interfered with.

It was nearing the end of August, and Dallas was definite about leaving. I got back on an airplane heading for Maryland and Jeremy's to get Dallas's car to drive to

Baltimore and pick him up. There had to be a meeting with the doctors before he checked out. They wanted him to stay longer because much more needed to be done to get his cognitive abilities back. They had given him a Day-Timer and instructed him to keep written track of his life and had set up outpatient times at a rehabilitation facility in the DC area. We checked him out and left for some shopping for new clothes and a haircut for Dallas and to check out where the outpatient facility was located and sign him up.

The next day, we went to the hospital to show him where he had been and to show the nurses how he was doing. After that reunion, we went to the scene of the accident so he could see the skid marks and maybe bring something to his memory. He still had no recollection of what had happened. Then we went to the beach in Ocean City, took pictures of him walking in the surf, and drove by Johnnie's Place. We had a really good time together. Dallas was going to stay at Jeremy's for a while and take the bus for his outpatient appointments. He was not to drive his car because his license was suspended until the court date. He did attend several sessions and seemed to continue improving, but one weekend in September, Jeremy called to say that Dallas had not come home and was found wandering around at a train station. We decided he needed to be home with us.

I had found a head injury/epilepsy group that met once a month in Janesville and had attended a few meetings and listened to others share their experiences with family members that had injuries similar to Dallas's. These meetings proved informative and comforting, and we also found an outpatient rehabilitation facility similar to the one in DC that Dallas could go to in eastern Wisconsin.

After his court appearance was over and he was given a duplicate license, Dallas drove home and resumed his rehabilitation; after about two months, he graduated. His status was guarded, regarding his short- term memory and higher executive thinking ability. There may be more improvement over time, but it would be slower and less noticeable. Many, many times, Dallas would come into my little office at home, and I would be at the computer working, and he would sit on the floor under the window close to my chair and talk.

There was anger in him that had not been there before the accident. He had a hard time remembering the right words to convey his thoughts. I would sit and listen and have a little input. It seemed he needed to be validated as thinking person.

As he tried to communicate, and I tried to comprehend, I remembered the prayer I had prayed before he was born, asking God to give me patience. Now, I had to put flesh on that gift and work it. So, I sat and listened and listened. If I could do anything but give him my time and listen and be a sounding board for him to learn how to put his thoughts together and learn how to express himself, that was what I needed to do for him at that time. I had to believe it was not wasted time, though my plans for my time were being delayed.

We hired Dallas to work for us, sweeping and mopping floors on some of our accounts for a couple of months to save money to try to go back to college. He wanted to continue his studies in international relations. He worked out the details and moved back in with his buddies and found a job a local TV station and tried school, but it just didn't work. The damage done to the area of his brain which controls short-term memory was interfering with his ability to keep up. It was not working out.

Then he came back home once again. The student loans were wasted, and the debt was still owed. He tried to get his life back to normal, but his normal wasn't mine. He did continue to go out almost every night to bars, where he could associate with others in his age group. I reasoned that his dad and I were his only family now; we were older, and he needed some outlet with friends. He didn't concern himself with the information the doctors had left him with that he shouldn't drink because of further damage to his brain. He knew he had lots of brain cells, and nothing like a glass of beer would impair him irreparably.

But it did impair him, and he did get stopped, usually late at night when bars closed and police knew people would be leaving these establishments under the influence. He got ticketed, once in Wisconsin and once in Illinois. I warned him that I wasn't going to take care of anything, even going to get him. The second time this happened in Illinois, he was carted off to jail and stayed there for a month because I would not bail him out. He had to sell his car to pay fines and the attorney he hired to plead his case.

This really jolted him; I thought he had come to his senses, especially after going to the classes they required and losing his beloved car. But not quite. It was much longer before he went out, and he did so less frequently, and he was being very, very careful. He was confident he could handle it. I had told him a while back that God must really love him a lot because He wasn't going to allow him to continue the lifestyle he was involved in and He would keep trying to get him to understand and to change.

A little over two years had passed since he had gotten out of jail when he was stopped leaving a downtown restaurant because he had pulled out of the parking space without the headlights on, just the parking lights. When asked to take a breathalyzer, he declined, and that resulted in a natural guilty by the law, and he was ticketed. This would be his fourth offense, and that makes it a felony here in Wisconsin. There are lots of consequences to a felony charge. You lose your right to vote or carry arms, amongst other things; Dallas knew he had gone too far on God's grace. He finally understood all he had lost because of alcohol, and he made the decision not to drink as he had in the past. He started going to substance abuse meetings on a weekly basis and paying $30 out of his own pocket each week. He was being his own judge and jury and paying the consequences for his actions. He has been faithful to his decision, and he has continued working for us in a larger capacity, doing a great job as a team leader. He has learned to be more frugal with his money and hopes to try school again in the future. His goals have changed, and now he is interested in human behavior.

The impact of the accident still goes on in all our lives. We work together each night cleaning a bank branch and have had the opportunity for many long and serious talks. These talks are more meaningful, and rarely does he have a hard time remembering the right words he wants to say. I can see real changes for the good in his life.

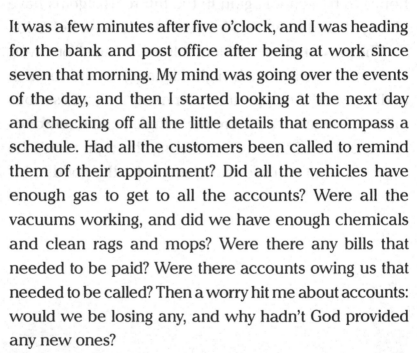

It was a few minutes after five o'clock, and I was heading for the bank and post office after being at work since seven that morning. My mind was going over the events of the day, and then I started looking at the next day and checking off all the little details that encompass a schedule. Had all the customers been called to remind them of their appointment? Did all the vehicles have enough gas to get to all the accounts? Were all the vacuums working, and did we have enough chemicals and clean rags and mops? Were there any bills that needed to be paid? Were there accounts owing us that needed to be called? Then a worry hit me about accounts: would we be losing any, and why hadn't God provided any new ones?

Then I was off on a worry binge. I had been asking God for added business to give employees more hours, and I hate to tread water. It seemed we had been at a standstill as far as adding new business for a while, and that can mean that we were not growing. We had not been actively marketing ourselves by going out and looking for new business for five years or so. I had decided to wait on the Lord for the right ones, in the right locations, with the right amount of work that we could perform correctly, since we had gotten ourselves in hot water a few times in the past by taking on business that was so far away and demanded good workers that were not at our disposal at the right time and adding more equipment. This trusting God to provide accounts was a blind walk of faith, and even if it seemed so last minute, over time, God had always provided.

But here I was, worrying. I was reminded that the guidebook had something to say about my thinking: "Be not conformed to the world's way of thinking, but be transformed by renewing your mind with God's thoughts."

I struggled to capture my thoughts. I discovered that I was not being content. I had wanting things to go my way, and that was causing me to worry and not be thankful. I had better start a list of things I was grateful for, right now, and I was challenging myself to see all God had given me, most unasked for and taken for granted; the listing continued till I was driving in my driveway because God is so good and so gracious.

Say you had to solve a computer glitch and you knew nothing about how a computer works, but you had a good friend you had known for many years and totally trusted him because he had been there for you in the past, and he was a computer geek and could accomplish miracles with computers. He had made a really big sacrifice in the past to get you out of a situation you were totally unable to do anything about. He had proved his love for you, and you could always call on him. If you had to move a big freezer and were in a wheelchair with a broken leg and had a good friend whose hobby was lifting weights and who was really strong, and you totally trusted him because he had made a great sacrifice years ago by giving up something precious to him to help you out, and you could call on him any time, what would you do?

I find myself in similar situations regularly. Because God is Spirit, and I can't see or feel or smell Him, I forget that He is there. He is always there, ready to help me out. He wants to help me out. If I just recognize His presence and willingness and capability and involve Him in my life, I have His help. God provides me many opportunities to use His help, and even when I do, I can still fall into a trap.

There was a luncheon way back in the early 1970s where I was in charge of introducing the speaker. I was nervous about my role, so I had prayed and asked God for His help. I even found a verse that morning in Psalms that stated "I sought the Lord and He delivered me from all my fears," so I felt confident that He was helping, and I promised that I would give Him the praise and glory for the result. When it was over, a guest came up to me and complimented me on the job I had done. The first words out of my mouth were thank you and then I mentioned something about the speaker. I had completely forgotten to mention the Lord; only hours later did it come to me that the Lord had been working for me, and I had forgotten to give Him the glory.

It is so easy to take credit. When I feel pretty good about passing a test or accomplishing something, there is an awareness that I am in deep waters and had better be careful. The second I become prideful, I am up for a fall. It is only by recognizing my weaknesses and faults and humbly seeking God's help and maintaining a thankful spirit that I can avoid the fall.

The garage door opened, and I slowly pulled into my parking place as the kitchen door swung open. Dallas was letting the dog out to welcome me. He angrily exclaimed that he wasn't going to take it anymore. Of course, I did not know what "it" was, but I guessed that he and his dad were into it. They occasionally bickered over the smallest of things because they were so much alike. Spencer came into the kitchen holding a light bulb, and both were talking at the same time, trying to get my attention. As I tried to get them to calm down, it encouraged each one to get louder and escalated into a yelling match. I left them and sat down on the sofa, hoping reason would prevail. Then Spencer came in with the light bulb, thinking he could explain. I said that I didn't want to hear a thing, and he turned away and walked out of the room. Then Dallas, who had gone to get his Bible to look up a passage to prove his point, approached me, and I told him that I didn't want to hear a thing. He, too, turned and walked away, and there was finally quiet.

I had heard a few phrases in the match, one of them being "honor your father" and one being "fathers don't provoke your children." They were using scripture against each other to prove their side of the issue, and it was falling on deaf ears. Scott was angry and hurt, and his dad was disgusted.

The next morning was a court appearance for Dallas. I had been taking him there for two years. I picked him up for the half-hour drive to Janesville, and he started talking about the fiasco from the night before.

I interrupted him and said, "You were wrong." He wouldn't hear of it and continued to explain his position, and I interrupted again, saying, "You were wrong."

He just couldn't see it. Why would God want him to respect a father who was provoking his child? It wasn't right, and he knew it. I told him the story in the Bible about King David and King Saul. God had taken the kingdom from Saul because of his disobedience but left him still in place. David had been chosen by God and anointed by the prophet, Samuel, and he knew the kingdom was his, but Saul still wore the crown. David had the chance to kill Saul during the long wait to actually sit on the throne, but he chose not to because he respected God's chain of command. Saul did not deserve that respect, but David gave it; God was pleased with David's humility and willingness to wait upon Him.

That seemed to get through to Dallas, but I went on to mention that we are told to respect all authority because it is ordained by God. It may not be good, but the position is to be honored, if not the person. I also mentioned that laws were allowed by God and respect was due them too, even seemingly trivial driving laws. He should relate to that because that was the reason we were driving to court. Then I continued to nail the lid on by telling Dallas that God told us to honor our bosses, even though they were not good bosses.

By the time we arrived, Dallas had a change of mind and was willing to admit that he had overstepped the boundaries and should ask for forgiveness. I knew the enemy of God's children had tried to throw Dallas a curveball just a few hours from court; he was trying to plant a seed of bitterness in him that would interfere with a clear conscience toward God and his father. It did give me a wonderful chance to bring home to Dallas a point that I had seen for while that needed correcting and had no opportunity as timely as this to share this doctrine with him.

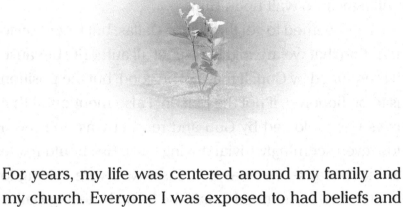

For years, my life was centered around my family and my church. Everyone I was exposed to had beliefs and lifestyles very similar to mine, and then the business became a part of my life, and I was introduced to people who did not attend church and knew nothing about God or His guidebook. Their world view was very different from mine. There was no one to share thoughts I had come away with from my quiet time or prayer requests. As a business owner, I had been warned that if I went too far in bringing religion to the workplace, I might be sued. In fact, one ex-employee who was suing me for unemployment insurance did bring up as part of his case against me that we had talked about religion at one time. Fortunately, he lost, but this incident made a big impression on me.

I brought some spiritual items to the office, and if anyone wanted to check them out, they could. There was a daily Bible reading and thought for the day on the counter and some verses scattered about, and there were occasions that came up in the daily routine that gave me opportunity to share scriptural principles. I discouraged foul language and gossiping and encouraged kindness and generosity and respect. Most everyone came to the conclusion that I believed in God, and they respected my desires.

Last year, one of the girls suggested we have a Bible study; using a study Bible for kids, we met in our office for an hour before a team was scheduled for work and did an overview of God's dealing with humankind from the beginning of creation to Israel's captivity and release through the shed blood of the Passover Lamb. Most of the information shared was brand new to the ones who came.

When summer arrived, it was impossible to continue, but at least some of God's Word got into them. There is a promise in the Bible that says that His Word will not return void. I know that the Word that was planted in my mind as a child worked to convict me of sin, judgment, and righteousness; like a powerful sword, it was able to separate the thoughts and intents of my heart and get me to the state of repentance from my own goodness and receive the gift of His life.

In 2009, after an eye exam for stronger glasses, the doctor told Spencer that he had macular degeneration in his one good eye; in order to deter the disease's progression, he needed to have a shot directly in the eye once a month. That went over big. Spencer loved to read and study and write, and seeing was essential. We didn't have to think too long to decide that the procedure had to be done. It looked worse than it actually was, though; sometimes, it took a day for his sight to get back to his normal. He tried many magnification glasses, but there was a limit to their effectiveness, and it became harder and harder for him to enjoy reading.

Some months later, he complained to me of a sharp pain behind his ear. We made an appointment with his doctor about a week later, and that was when we discovered that he had a growth on his thyroid gland; this growth was pressing on a nerve, causing the pain. After some tests, we were told that it was cancer, and the best place to go for that was a hospital in Madison.

We began researching and found a surgeon known for thyroid procedures and made an appointment. This was in September 2013, as Spencer turned eighty-one, and there were more tests and a CT scan to determine if the cancer had spread. There was no evidence of spreading, and after this new doctor had finished with his examinations, he agreed that surgery was the best way to proceed. I pushed for the surgery to take place quickly, so there would be little chance for the cancer to spread further.

The surgery was scheduled for January 2, 2014. Spencer and I held onto each other. We were both adjusting to this new set of circumstances. He had painted a picture in my mind years before of the two of us sitting in rocking chairs on our front porch when we were old and just enjoying each other. Was that ever to be? Did God have something else in mind?

The expense of the surgery and hospital and doctors loomed before us. I reassured my hubby that if we could use our line of credit on our home for a new roof, which we had done the year before, then, for sure, we could dip into the line for him.

Christy and Bruce became involved, and as the New Year approached, we all prayed for good weather for the forty-five-minute drive to Madison on New Year's Day for us and the three-hour drive from Iowa for Christy and

Bruce. It was cold and crisp, and light snow was falling, but the drive was good for both of us.

The doctor was going to remove the whole thyroid gland and the voice box and leave Spencer with a stoma. This would mean that he would be breathing through a hole in his neck and would have to learn to talk with a device held against his throat. This man who loved to read and study and share and teach and preach was now going to be in a place that would limit the activities that gave him joy and satisfaction. This was a hurdle. He courageously faced the future and trusted his Father God.

The four of us drove to the hospital early, and Spencer was admitted and went to the pre-surgery area to be prepped. There were a few tears when we were allowed in and more when they wheeled him out. During the five-hour surgery, we sat downstairs in a large waiting room, praying silently. After the doctor came to tell us it was over, we went in to see him. I would have to learn how to do the regular maintenance on the stoma and how to change the feeding bag on his tube. The hospital put a cot next to Spencer's bed for me to be able to stay close by him and be able to check on him during the night. He had a feeding tube in his nose and a needle in his arm and a cover over the stoma.

Later, he was encouraged to get up and walk for short distances. His spirits were good, and he was adjusting gradually. For a man who had not even seen a doctor for forty years, he was taking it in good stride. He lost quite a bit of weight during those first days, and when we headed home, he was looking forward to a good cup of coffee and maybe a biscuit. The biscuit was to be some time away, but the coffee was going to be a treat.

Come to find out, when you are not breathing through your nose, the sense of smell is gone, and the sense of taste is lessened, so the cup of coffee was really a big disappointment. He loved his coffee and drank several cups a day, always with four spoons of sugar. One other thing added on to the hurdle, and one more thing to subtract from satisfaction. He could not eat for a week or so because of the stitches inside his throat, so I would leave work to place his lunch bag on the feeding tube.

A checkup appointment in Madison proved he was okay, and the tube was removed. Then he could eat soft, smooth food and drink most anything. Although he was quite particular about his food, and "different" was the word he would use if my cooking wasn't up to par, he began gaining weight, and in March, he began the radiation therapy once a week. He tried to learn to speak with the device but found a whiteboard was easier to communicate with.

We would take short walks, and occasionally, visitors would come by, and the kids took time from their lives and visited.

In July, he was scheduled for a one-time irradiated iodine capsule and had to limit iodine in his diet for a month prior. I found that most foods contain iodine and had to really look hard at all I was preparing for his meals. Before taking the capsule, an x-ray showed that there were three or four small possibly cancerous tumors in his lung, but they said if these were cells from his thyroid, the irradiated iodine would kill them.

After he took the capsule, I was to stay at least an arm' s-length away from him for three days. I moved into the guest bedroom and used the main bathroom and hurriedly did the maintenance on his stoma and blew him kisses.

Later in July, he began having upset stomachs and diarrhea and losing weight. He tired easily and wouldn't go for a walk with me; he wasn't hungry and was not interested in too much. The kids and grandkids visited, and there was some spark for a while, but it took more effort for him.

I felt I should be with him more and looked into selling our company. I checked out the Yellow Pages and found four firms in our area that I thought might want to acquire our company. There was some interest, but because we were a commercial and residential cleaning company, most firms were only interested in buying our equipment. It seems that residential service is more costly for insurance and transportation. I gave up on that and decided to just keep going.

Our son Andrew came to visit his dad in early September. On Sunday morning, I noticed Spencer's abdomen looked distended, and the first thought that came to me was a blockage. It was a good thing Andrew was home because I couldn't have gotten Spencer to the car alone. Between the two of us, we managed and quickly got to the emergency room after a call to Madison.

Blood and urine work was ordered, and it was found that it was his bladder that was causing the swelling of his abdomen. He was admitted. There was an infection somewhere and antibiotics were begun. The family was called. Monday saw me driving to work and to the hospital and back home, and that would become my routine for over a week. I was so thankful that I had something to do. I had to be at work every morning. I had to schedule the appointments and get the supplies and equipment ready for each team to take. I had to pay bills and do payroll and do the laundry. If I was not concentrating on these things, I might have fallen into the worry trap or begun to feel sorry for myself.

I was sleeping alone and cooking for one and watching the TV shows I wanted to watch, but it was not fun. I remembered once when I was a little girl, and all I thought about was fun.

My dad had asked me to do something, and I told him that it was not fun, and he said back to me, "Daughter, life is not all fun. There are some un-funny things that are a part of life."

"Yes, Daddy."

I continued to be most grateful for the father God gave me because he gave of himself to his family and was a great representative of our heavenly Father God. It has made it easier to trust Him, because my earthly father was loving and trustworthy.

The doctors suggested Spencer be given morphine, but I resisted because it felt so final. After the nurse and the family kept telling me that it would be in his best interests, I relented. He rested easier after that and had moments when we could communicate, but most of the time, he slept. Hospice had been notified, and they followed up on brochures regarding grief.

Andrew had to go home, but Christy and Gordon made sure they were there with me and their father. One Wednesday, Gordon called while I was at work and said that I should get to the hospital quickly. I left the office and sped to his room, but just moments before I got there, he had gone to his heavenly Father.

I said, "Oh, my dear," bent over the rail, and gave my husband a last tearful kiss good-bye.

The house his soul and spirit had lived in was now vacant. He was home, finally, and singing some Hallelujahs (probably off-key).

This time, my hospital experience was different than with Dallas. I did not feel vulnerable. Of course, it was different because Spencer was older than Dallas and had lived a very full life. We had been given over fifty years together and had five wonderful children and twelve super grandchildren. Spencer had worked on a bus ministry for the church and taught Bible classes and preached and witnessed to anyone he could. He had been bold.

One time, a friend who was married to a man she thought was not saved asked Spencer to talk to him. He was in the hospital and it looked serious, and she was concerned for him. After a two-hour visit, Spencer came home upset. He had gone over passages in the Bible that explained our need for forgiveness and God's provision through His Son, the Messiah, Jesus, and had asked for a decision. He was rebuffed several times. This man could see his need. He said so. He could see that God was a forgiving God, and he could see what Jesus had done, but he could not and would not forgive himself. All we could do was to pray for him.

After his dad died, Jeremy came home to help any way he could. We were in the kitchen, waiting on the microwave to finish warming a cup of coffee, and he asked me some question about God and His sovereignty. I answered in the most scientific way I could because he is an engineer and thinks in facts and logic; I explained how God is always in the now. He is above time; in fact, He created time. It is always now with God. He is always in the past, He is always in the present, and He is always in the future. He knows all and is never surprised; because He is everywhere all the time, He controls everything, and His timing is always perfect. That gave him something to think about.

Gordon and I made all the final arrangements at the funeral home. All the paperwork, announcements, and notifications were taken care of. I decided not to have a service at that time but to wait because there had been so much traveling back and forth the past months by the kids. A later time seemed best to celebrate Spencer's life. I checked out several locations and decided upon the Angel Museum. It had been a church many years ago, with a basement fitted for groups. The date was set for December 6, and when the day arrived, the weather was beautiful. With much help from Christy and Bruce and Andrew's wife, Becky, we had food and drink and a TV to watch the video the funeral home had made using the many pictures the grandkids had picked out from our large collection. There were many friends from churches we had attended and Bible studies we had been involved in, and many of our employees came. We reminisced and laughed and renewed relationships that time had made inconsequential; Spencer would have really enjoyed it.

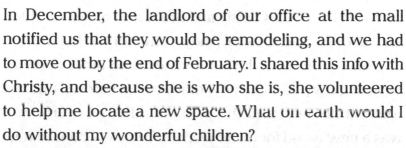

In December, the landlord of our office at the mall notified us that they would be remodeling, and we had to move out by the end of February. I shared this info with Christy, and because she is who she is, she volunteered to help me locate a new space. What on earth would I do without my wonderful children?

We were driving around one Saturday while checking out the internet and happened to notice a sign at the end of a small strip mall of a space available. We pulled into the parking lot and looked through the windows; the space seemed a pretty good size, and we called the number. The landlady arrived a few minutes later and opened the door. It looked beautiful to me, even though it was dirty and there were mirrors on the wall (it had been a beauty salon); it even had a washer and dryer.

No more searching, no more thought; we handed over a check for February's rent and signed the lease. Bruce made plans to bring his sons and remove all the sinks and mirrors and to paint. We all pitched in, and within a few days, somehow it became Clean Sweep Company. There was so much equipment stored in our old office that we hadn't used; we needed to get rid of them, but how? There was an auction house in our town, and we found out they would move all the items to their place and hold an auction, so that was the best way to handle all the stuff. Of course, they would take a percentage of the sales.

Boxes were collected and quickly filled, and the dumpster out back was packed with outdated, broken items and old files. Christy and Bruce and Shawn and Jon and Andrew and his son, Andy, came for the big moving day, and several employees donated their time. God was directing my path. The new office had windows, and the roof did not leak and the plumbing did not overflow. It was a new world for me to work in. Two new commercial contracts came in; we were seeing growth again. Things were going well, and I was able to keep up with the ordering of supplies and the scheduling and paying our bills on time. We were smaller but more efficient.

The biggest problem was that there was no one to do the marketing. I could not leave the office for any length of time to make calls, and even though we were in a more visible space, not enough businesses could see us. I could not come up with a plan that would work; Christy had wanted to work up some brochures for me, but she had been having problems at her own job, so she couldn't follow through. I was just putzing along.

In September, Gordon came from Virginia for a visit to check on his mom. He had been a project manager and knew a lot about business; unawares to me, he was assessing mine.

Around Thanksgiving, he called me while I was at work and said, "Mom, I have a job for you to do."

I couldn't imagine what it could be with the distance between us, except for praying, and he knew I did that. Way back when Jeremy went to the university an NROTC scholarship, I had the idea that since there were five days in a week, and I had five kids, I could designate one day as a special day for each one. I may not have known everything that was happening to my children, but God did, and I could be specific in praying for them. Gordon knew Thursday was his day.

I answered back, "What is that?"

He said that he wanted me to pack up my duds and move in with him. I must admit I might have been playing computer solitaire, because I did that when things were slow, so I stopped and asked him to repeat what he had just said. I was surprised. This was a new idea. I thanked him for his concern and love and told him I would think on it and pray about it.

Some excitement began building inside me. I told no one. I did think about it lots, trying to figure how it might happen, and I did pray about it. It was getting close to Christmas, and Christy called to check out plans for the holiday. Something led me to mention Gordon's offer to her. She informed me that she knew all about it. Gordon had talked with her before he had called me, and she had told him that she thought it was a good idea.

That settled it for me, and that very afternoon, I called Gordon and asked if his offer was still good. He laughed and said yes. I started making lists and told Dallas what was going to happen.

Considering our contracts and dealing with payroll kept my mind busy; it seemed best to make January 2016 our last month in business. There would have to be enough notice to our employees to give them time to look for a job, and all accounts would have to be notified. We offered our equipment to other cleaning companies, and the landlady was called. When February began, I was at work, finishing the last payroll and receiving payments for work done and making more lists. These were things that had to be done for the business to finish. There were a few pieces of equipment that other cleaning companies bought, and Dallas and I took several car loads of what was not sold to the Goodwill store, and after taking out the garbage and sweeping the floor, I locked the door and left the key for the landlady. Then it was time to work on our house.

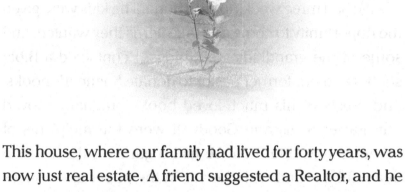

This house, where our family had lived for forty years, was now just real estate. A friend suggested a Realtor, and he walked through the house and made some suggestions; we agreed on a figure and decided to put it on the market in April. There was no time to get sentimental over the rooms where studying and eating and arguments and fellowship had taken place. We had to get it ready for new owners to live.

Repairs and deep cleaning and painting and getting rid of stuff and deciding what we needed to take east was the work ahead of us. Chuck, Gordon's son, was out of work and had been living with him. I asked if he would give us a hand with all the work and help with the drive to Virginia. I just knew that with Dallas driving the truck and me driving the car all that way, it would not be good. Chuck could drive one, and Dallas could drive the other, and I could help if needed.

Chuck jumped at the idea and arrived in early April.

What a help he was with the painting and packing. The great add-on was that we got to know each other. He had been a little boy the last time we were together, and now he was twenty-one.

We had three weeks to get it done. The kids were given the opportunity to come and take items they wanted, and some of the grandkids took things. I contacted a Bible school and our former pastor to donate Spencer's books, and boxes of his much-loved books gradually moved out. Easter Seals and Goodwill were the recipients of several loads, and then we had a garage sale. It was a beautiful day and with the ads in the paper and notices tacked to telephone poles, we had many flocking to see what bargains they could fine. Everything sold out pretty quickly, and the driveway was soon bare. I would not think about these things as something my husband and I had collected together. My life was on a different path, and I had to pack for this path. All this was just stuff, and I was not going to use it; maybe someone else could.

I had recognized the struggle with greed in my life some time back. There was little evidence of this problem, because there was never enough money for me to satisfy my wants. There was barely enough to take care of the needs while raising five children. But I really didn't like to go shopping with friends, because I could want so much. Spencer was the shopper. He could just look and look and compare quality against quality and price against price objectively. I was emotionally attached right away to things that caught my eye.

Of the big three, the lust of the eye, the lust of the flesh, and the pride of life, the one that fit me was the lust of the eye. I didn't see much harm when I had no funds, but God did. It struck me hard when I really understood what God meant when He said that greed is like the sin of idolatry and rebellion is as the sin of witchcraft. Even though I couldn't afford something, if I let the desire rule, I was in trouble. God looks at the heart and He deserves the first place in the list of the desires of our heart. So, when the time came to let go of things, it was not hard to do.

Sunday, April 17, we were loading the truck we had rented. With the help of Christy and Bruce and Chuck, we packed it full. About eight o'clock, we turned the lights off at the old homestead and locked the doors and began our journey east. Wow! Somehow, we had managed to get everything done. Chuck drove the truck, and Dallas and I were in my car. On Monday night, really Tuesday morning, at one o'clock, we drove into Gordon's driveway.

The house sold three days after going on the market and for more than what we had listed it for. Spencer would have been pleased.

The process that transforms a tree into a diamond was brought to my attention several years ago, and I was affected by the long, arduous manner that produced the valuable stone. During the flood in Noah's day, trees were uprooted, animals and people died, and as the water receded and mud slides and disturbances of the earth's surface took place, dead trees were buried under tons of wet earth. Over time, this wood turned into coal under the heat and pressure developing. More time and more pressure and more heat, and gradually a stone was formed. It struck me that I could liken myself as a tree, and if I desired to be transformed into something more valuable, I would have to undergo the process. I might as well find some joy in it.

To this point, I have become more and more impressed with the relationship creator God desires. He has gone to extreme measures to establish the means by which the beings He created can know Him. He is the lover of my soul, which promotes the intimacy between lovers. He is my heavenly Father and seeks involvement in my life as counselor and adviser. He is my dearest friend and wants to talk with me and listen to all I have to say.

As I move through life, each step is an opportunity to tap into each facet of the relationship that began the instant I believed. This process is precious. It is the treasure. It is the abundant life promised to a child of God.

Printed in the United States
By Bookmasters